50 Summer Feast Recipes for Home

By: Kelly Johnson

Table of Contents

- Grilled Lemon Herb Chicken
- Watermelon Feta Salad
- Barbecue Ribs
- Caprese Skewers
- Shrimp Tacos
- Corn on the Cob with Chili Lime Butter
- Strawberry Spinach Salad
- Grilled Swordfish with Mango Salsa
- Greek Orzo Salad
- Pulled Pork Sandwiches
- Pesto Pasta Salad
- Teriyaki Beef Kebabs
- Gazpacho
- Grilled Portobello Mushrooms
- Pineapple Chicken Kabobs
- Cucumber Mint Salad
- Fish Tacos with Chipotle Crema
- Tomato Basil Bruschetta
- Grilled Vegetable Platter
- Mango Coconut Rice
- Lemon Garlic Shrimp Scampi
- Avocado Corn Salad
- Hawaiian Pork Sliders
- Mediterranean Stuffed Bell Peppers
- Grilled Eggplant with Tahini Sauce
- Berry Salad with Poppyseed Dressing
- Thai Peanut Noodles
- Citrus Marinated Salmon
- Caesar Salad with Grilled Chicken
- Black Bean and Corn Salsa
- Spicy Grilled Sausages
- Ratatouille
- Pesto Grilled Cheese
- Melon Prosciutto Skewers
- Chicken Caesar Wraps
- Quinoa Tabbouleh

- Teriyaki Salmon Burgers
- Blueberry Crumble Bars
- Cornbread Muffins
- Lemon Herb Grilled Zucchini
- Watermelon Mint Cooler
- Mediterranean Chickpea Salad
- Honey Lime Chicken Wings
- Stuffed Jalapeños
- Grilled Flatbread with Hummus
- Summer Berry Trifle
- BBQ Chicken Pizza
- Key Lime Pie
- Peach Cobbler
- Strawberry Shortcake

Grilled Lemon Herb Chicken

Ingredients:

- 4 boneless, skinless chicken breasts
- 2 lemons, juiced and zested
- 3-4 garlic cloves, minced
- 2 tablespoons fresh chopped herbs (such as rosemary, thyme, or oregano)
- 1/4 cup olive oil
- Salt and pepper, to taste

Instructions:

Prepare the Marinade:
- In a bowl, whisk together the lemon juice, lemon zest, minced garlic, chopped herbs, olive oil, salt, and pepper.

Marinate the Chicken:
- Place the chicken breasts in a shallow dish or a resealable plastic bag.
- Pour the marinade over the chicken, making sure each piece is well coated.
- Cover the dish or seal the bag and refrigerate for at least 30 minutes (or up to 4 hours) to allow the flavors to infuse.

Preheat the Grill:
- Preheat your grill to medium-high heat (about 375-400°F / 190-200°C).

Grill the Chicken:
- Remove the chicken from the marinade, shaking off any excess.
- Place the chicken breasts on the grill and discard the remaining marinade.
- Grill the chicken for about 6-8 minutes per side, or until the internal temperature reaches 165°F (75°C) and the chicken is cooked through. The exact grilling time will depend on the thickness of your chicken breasts.

Rest and Serve:
- Once cooked, transfer the grilled chicken to a plate and let it rest for a few minutes.
- Slice the chicken, if desired, and serve with additional lemon wedges on the side.

Enjoy!
- Serve the Grilled Lemon Herb Chicken with your favorite summer sides like grilled vegetables, salads, or rice.

This Grilled Lemon Herb Chicken recipe is perfect for summer gatherings and pairs beautifully with fresh seasonal ingredients. Adjust the herbs and seasonings according to your taste preferences for a personalized touch.

Watermelon Feta Salad

Ingredients:

- 4 cups cubed seedless watermelon
- 1 cup crumbled feta cheese
- 1/4 cup fresh mint leaves, thinly sliced
- 2 tablespoons extra virgin olive oil
- 1 tablespoon fresh lime juice
- Salt and pepper, to taste
- Optional: sliced red onion or black olives for additional flavor

Instructions:

Prepare the Watermelon:
- Cut the seedless watermelon into bite-sized cubes, removing any seeds. Place the watermelon cubes in a large mixing bowl.

Add the Feta and Mint:
- Crumble the feta cheese over the watermelon cubes.
- Tear or thinly slice the fresh mint leaves and add them to the bowl.

Dress the Salad:
- In a small bowl, whisk together the extra virgin olive oil and fresh lime juice.
- Drizzle the dressing over the watermelon, feta, and mint.
- Gently toss the salad to coat all the ingredients evenly.

Season and Serve:
- Season the Watermelon Feta Salad with a pinch of salt and pepper, to taste.
- Optionally, add some sliced red onion or black olives for extra flavor and texture.

Chill and Enjoy:
- Refrigerate the salad for about 15-30 minutes to allow the flavors to meld together and chill.
- Serve the Watermelon Feta Salad chilled as a refreshing side dish or appetizer.

Serve Suggestions:
- This salad pairs wonderfully with grilled meats or seafood, making it a perfect addition to summer barbecues or picnics.
- Garnish with additional fresh mint leaves or lime wedges before serving.

Enjoy this Watermelon Feta Salad as a light and delightful summer dish that captures the essence of the season with its sweet, savory, and tangy flavors!

Barbecue Ribs

Ingredients:

- 2 racks of pork baby back ribs (about 4-5 pounds total)
- Salt and black pepper, to taste
- 1 cup barbecue sauce (homemade or store-bought)
- Optional: additional barbecue rub or seasoning blend for extra flavor

Instructions:

Prep the Ribs:
- Start by removing the membrane from the back of the ribs. Use a butter knife or your fingers to loosen and lift one corner of the membrane. Once loosened, grab the membrane with a paper towel and pull it off completely. This step helps the ribs become more tender.

Season the Ribs:
- Season the racks of ribs generously with salt and black pepper on both sides. Optionally, apply a barbecue rub or seasoning blend for extra flavor. Rub the seasonings into the meat.

Prepare the Grill (or Oven):
- If using a grill: Preheat your grill to medium heat (around 300-325°F / 150-160°C) for indirect cooking. Set up the grill for indirect heat by turning off burners on one side (if using a gas grill) or arranging charcoal to one side (if using a charcoal grill).
- If using an oven: Preheat your oven to 300°F (150°C).

Cooking the Ribs:
- Place the seasoned ribs on the grill or in the oven, bone-side down, away from direct heat. If using a grill, close the lid.
- Cook the ribs low and slow for about 2.5 to 3 hours, or until the meat is tender and begins to pull away from the bones. You can rotate or flip the ribs halfway through cooking for even doneness.

Apply Barbecue Sauce:
- During the last 30 minutes of cooking, start basting the ribs with your favorite barbecue sauce. Brush a generous amount of sauce over the ribs, allowing it to caramelize and develop a nice glaze.
- Apply additional layers of barbecue sauce every 10 minutes or so, building up a flavorful coating.

Rest and Serve:

- Once the ribs are done cooking and beautifully glazed, remove them from the grill or oven.
- Let the ribs rest for a few minutes before slicing them into individual portions.

Enjoy!

- Serve the barbecue ribs hot with extra barbecue sauce on the side. Pair them with coleslaw, cornbread, baked beans, or your favorite summer sides.

This recipe will yield deliciously tender and flavorful barbecue ribs that are sure to be a hit at any summer feast or barbecue gathering. Adjust cooking times and temperatures based on your equipment and desired level of doneness. Enjoy!

Caprese Skewers

Ingredients:

- Cherry or grape tomatoes
- Fresh mozzarella balls (also known as bocconcini)
- Fresh basil leaves
- Balsamic glaze (or balsamic reduction)
- Wooden skewers (6-inch or cocktail picks)

Instructions:

Prepare Ingredients:
- Rinse the cherry or grape tomatoes and pat them dry with a paper towel.
- Drain the fresh mozzarella balls if they are stored in liquid.
- Pick fresh basil leaves from the stems and wash them gently. Pat them dry with a paper towel.

Assemble the Skewers:
- Take a wooden skewer or cocktail pick and start assembling the Caprese skewers.
- Thread one cherry tomato onto the skewer.
- Follow with a fresh mozzarella ball.
- Add a folded basil leaf next to the mozzarella.
- Repeat this pattern (tomato, mozzarella, basil) until the skewer is filled, leaving a small space at the end for easy handling.

Arrange and Serve:
- Place the assembled Caprese skewers on a serving platter or plate.
- Drizzle balsamic glaze over the skewers just before serving. If you don't have balsamic glaze, you can use a balsamic reduction or simply a high-quality balsamic vinegar.

Optional Variations:
- You can customize your Caprese skewers by adding additional ingredients such as marinated olives, grilled vegetables (like zucchini or bell peppers), or prosciutto for a more substantial appetizer.

Enjoy!
- Serve the Caprese skewers as a colorful and flavorful appetizer at your summer feast or party.
- These skewers can be made ahead of time and stored in the refrigerator until ready to serve.

Caprese skewers are not only delicious but also visually appealing, making them a perfect addition to any summer gathering. Enjoy the combination of juicy tomatoes, creamy mozzarella, fragrant basil, and tangy balsamic glaze in every bite!

Shrimp Tacos

Ingredients:

For the Shrimp:

- 1 pound large shrimp, peeled and deveined
- 2 tablespoons olive oil
- 2 cloves garlic, minced
- 1 teaspoon chili powder
- 1/2 teaspoon cumin
- Salt and pepper, to taste
- Juice of 1 lime

For Serving:

- Corn or flour tortillas (8-10, small size)
- Shredded cabbage or lettuce
- Diced tomatoes
- Sliced avocado or guacamole
- Chopped fresh cilantro
- Sliced jalapeños (optional)
- Sour cream or Mexican crema
- Lime wedges

Instructions:

Prepare the Shrimp:
- In a bowl, combine the peeled and deveined shrimp with olive oil, minced garlic, chili powder, cumin, salt, pepper, and lime juice. Toss to coat the shrimp evenly.

Cook the Shrimp:
- Heat a large skillet or grill pan over medium-high heat.
- Add the seasoned shrimp to the hot skillet in a single layer.
- Cook the shrimp for 2-3 minutes per side, or until they are pink and opaque. Be careful not to overcook the shrimp as they can become rubbery.

Warm the Tortillas:

- While the shrimp is cooking, warm the tortillas. You can heat them in a dry skillet for about 30 seconds on each side or wrap them in foil and warm them in the oven for a few minutes.

Assemble the Tacos:
- Once the shrimp are cooked, it's time to assemble the tacos.
- Place a few shrimp onto each tortilla.
- Top the shrimp with shredded cabbage or lettuce, diced tomatoes, sliced avocado or guacamole, chopped cilantro, and sliced jalapeños (if using).
- Drizzle with sour cream or Mexican crema.
- Squeeze fresh lime juice over the tacos for a burst of flavor.

Serve and Enjoy:
- Serve the shrimp tacos immediately while warm.
- Offer lime wedges on the side for additional squeezing.
- Enjoy these delicious shrimp tacos with your favorite summer sides like Mexican rice, black beans, or a fresh corn salad.

Feel free to customize these shrimp tacos with your favorite toppings and condiments. They make a delightful main dish for any summer gathering, providing a taste of coastal flavors in every bite. Adjust the seasoning levels and spice according to your preferences. Enjoy your homemade shrimp tacos!

Corn on the Cob with Chili Lime Butter

Ingredients:

- 4 ears of corn, husked
- 4 tablespoons unsalted butter, softened
- Zest of 1 lime
- 1 tablespoon lime juice
- 1 teaspoon chili powder
- 1/2 teaspoon smoked paprika (optional)
- Salt, to taste
- Chopped fresh cilantro (for garnish, optional)

Instructions:

Prepare the Corn:
- Start by husking the ears of corn and removing any silk.
- Rinse the corn under cold water and pat dry with paper towels.

Make the Chili Lime Butter:
- In a small bowl, combine the softened butter, lime zest, lime juice, chili powder, smoked paprika (if using), and a pinch of salt.
- Mix everything together until well combined. Taste and adjust the seasoning if needed.

Grill or Boil the Corn:
- Grilling method: Preheat your grill to medium-high heat. Place the corn directly on the grill grates and cook, turning occasionally, until the corn is charred in spots and tender, about 10-12 minutes.
- Boiling method: Bring a large pot of salted water to a boil. Add the husked corn and boil for about 5-7 minutes until the corn is tender.

Apply the Chili Lime Butter:
- Once the corn is cooked, remove it from the grill or pot.
- Using a butter knife or pastry brush, generously spread the chili lime butter over each ear of corn while it's still hot. Make sure to coat the corn evenly with the butter mixture.

Serve and Garnish:
- Place the buttered corn on a serving platter.
- Sprinkle chopped fresh cilantro over the corn for garnish, if desired.

Enjoy!
- Serve the chili lime buttered corn on the cob immediately while warm.

- Optionally, provide extra lime wedges on the side for squeezing over the corn before eating.

This corn on the cob with chili lime butter is bursting with flavor and makes a fantastic side dish for any summer meal, especially when served alongside grilled meats or seafood. It's a crowd-pleaser that's easy to prepare and will surely impress your guests! Adjust the amount of chili powder based on your spice preference. Enjoy your deliciously seasoned corn on the cob!

Strawberry Spinach Salad

Ingredients:

For the Salad:

- 6 cups fresh baby spinach leaves
- 1 pint (about 2 cups) fresh strawberries, hulled and sliced
- 1/4 cup sliced almonds or chopped pecans
- Optional: crumbled feta cheese or goat cheese

For the Dressing:

- 1/4 cup extra virgin olive oil
- 2 tablespoons balsamic vinegar
- 1 tablespoon honey or maple syrup
- 1 teaspoon Dijon mustard
- Salt and pepper, to taste

Instructions:

Prepare the Salad Ingredients:
- Rinse the baby spinach leaves thoroughly and pat them dry with paper towels or a salad spinner.
- Hull the strawberries (remove stems) and slice them into thin rounds.
- If using nuts, toast them lightly in a dry skillet over medium heat until fragrant and golden. Set aside to cool.

Assemble the Salad:
- In a large salad bowl, combine the baby spinach, sliced strawberries, and toasted nuts.
- If desired, sprinkle crumbled feta cheese or goat cheese over the salad ingredients.

Make the Dressing:
- In a small bowl or jar, whisk together the extra virgin olive oil, balsamic vinegar, honey or maple syrup, Dijon mustard, salt, and pepper until well combined.

Toss and Serve:
- Just before serving, drizzle the dressing over the strawberry spinach salad.

- Gently toss the salad to coat the ingredients evenly with the dressing. Enjoy!
    - Serve the strawberry spinach salad immediately as a refreshing side dish or light meal.
    - This salad pairs well with grilled chicken, salmon, or crusty bread.

Feel free to customize this salad by adding other ingredients like avocado slices, red onion, or cooked quinoa for extra texture and flavor. The combination of sweet strawberries, tender spinach, crunchy nuts, and tangy dressing makes this strawberry spinach salad a delicious and healthy addition to any summer feast. Enjoy the burst of flavors in every bite! Adjust the sweetness and tanginess of the dressing according to your taste preferences.

Grilled Swordfish with Mango Salsa

Ingredients:

For the Grilled Swordfish:

- 4 swordfish steaks (6-8 ounces each), about 1-inch thick
- 2 tablespoons olive oil
- Salt and pepper, to taste
- 1 teaspoon paprika
- 1/2 teaspoon garlic powder
- 1/2 teaspoon dried oregano
- 1/2 teaspoon ground cumin
- Juice of 1 lime

For the Mango Salsa:

- 1 ripe mango, peeled, pitted, and diced
- 1/2 red bell pepper, diced
- 1/4 red onion, finely chopped
- 1 jalapeño pepper, seeded and minced (optional)
- 2 tablespoons chopped fresh cilantro
- Juice of 1 lime
- Salt and pepper, to taste

Instructions:

Prepare the Swordfish:
- Pat dry the swordfish steaks with paper towels.
- In a small bowl, combine olive oil, salt, pepper, paprika, garlic powder, dried oregano, ground cumin, and lime juice to make a marinade.
- Rub the marinade all over the swordfish steaks. Let them marinate for about 15-30 minutes at room temperature while you prepare the mango salsa.

Make the Mango Salsa:
- In a medium bowl, combine diced mango, diced red bell pepper, finely chopped red onion, minced jalapeño (if using), chopped fresh cilantro, lime juice, salt, and pepper.

- Mix well to combine. Taste and adjust seasoning according to your preference. Set aside.

Grill the Swordfish:
- Preheat your grill to medium-high heat.
- Place the marinated swordfish steaks on the grill and cook for about 4-5 minutes per side, or until the fish is opaque and easily flakes with a fork. Cooking time may vary depending on the thickness of the steaks.

Serve:
- Once the swordfish is cooked through, transfer the steaks to a serving platter.
- Spoon the mango salsa over the grilled swordfish steaks.
- Garnish with additional fresh cilantro and lime wedges if desired.

Enjoy!
- Serve the grilled swordfish with mango salsa immediately.
- This dish pairs well with rice, quinoa, or a side salad for a complete meal.

Grilled swordfish with mango salsa is a flavorful and vibrant dish that's sure to impress your guests at any summer gathering. The combination of juicy swordfish and sweet-spicy mango salsa creates a perfect harmony of flavors. Enjoy this tropical delight! Adjust the level of spiciness in the mango salsa by adding more or less jalapeño according to your preference.

Greek Orzo Salad

Ingredients:

For the Salad:

- 1 ½ cups orzo pasta
- 1 English cucumber, diced
- 1 pint cherry tomatoes, halved
- 1/2 red onion, finely chopped
- 1/2 cup Kalamata olives, pitted and sliced
- 1/2 cup crumbled feta cheese
- 1/4 cup chopped fresh parsley
- 1/4 cup chopped fresh dill (or 1 tablespoon dried dill)
- Salt and black pepper, to taste

For the Dressing:

- 1/4 cup extra virgin olive oil
- 3 tablespoons red wine vinegar
- 1 tablespoon lemon juice
- 1 teaspoon Dijon mustard
- 1 garlic clove, minced
- 1 teaspoon dried oregano
- Salt and black pepper, to taste

Instructions:

Cook the Orzo:
- Bring a large pot of salted water to a boil. Add the orzo pasta and cook according to package instructions until al dente. Drain the orzo and rinse under cold water to stop the cooking process. Drain well and transfer to a large mixing bowl.

Prepare the Salad Ingredients:
- Add the diced cucumber, halved cherry tomatoes, chopped red onion, sliced Kalamata olives, crumbled feta cheese, chopped parsley, and chopped dill to the bowl with the cooked orzo.

Make the Dressing:

- In a small bowl or jar, whisk together the extra virgin olive oil, red wine vinegar, lemon juice, Dijon mustard, minced garlic, dried oregano, salt, and black pepper until well combined.

Assemble the Salad:
- Pour the dressing over the orzo and vegetables in the mixing bowl.
- Toss everything together until the salad is well coated with the dressing.
- Taste and adjust seasoning with additional salt and pepper if needed.

Chill and Serve:
- Cover the Greek orzo salad and refrigerate for at least 1 hour to allow the flavors to meld together.
- Before serving, give the salad a final toss and adjust seasoning if necessary.

Enjoy!
- Serve the Greek orzo salad chilled as a delicious side dish or light main course.
- Garnish with additional fresh herbs or crumbled feta cheese before serving, if desired.

This Greek orzo salad is bursting with Mediterranean flavors and makes a perfect addition to any summer feast or picnic. It's colorful, flavorful, and satisfying, showcasing the best of Greek cuisine with fresh ingredients and a zesty dressing. Enjoy this refreshing salad with family and friends! Feel free to customize the salad by adding more vegetables or herbs according to your taste preferences.

Pulled Pork Sandwiches

Ingredients:

For the Pulled Pork:

- 3-4 pounds pork shoulder (also known as pork butt), boneless
- 2 tablespoons brown sugar
- 2 teaspoons salt
- 1 teaspoon black pepper
- 1 teaspoon paprika
- 1 teaspoon garlic powder
- 1 teaspoon onion powder
- 1/2 teaspoon dried thyme
- 1/2 teaspoon dried oregano
- 1/4 teaspoon cayenne pepper (adjust to taste)
- 1 cup chicken or vegetable broth
- 1 cup barbecue sauce (plus extra for serving)
- Hamburger buns or sandwich rolls

For Serving:

- Coleslaw (optional, for topping)
- Pickles (optional, for serving)

Instructions:

Prepare the Pork:
- In a small bowl, mix together the brown sugar, salt, black pepper, paprika, garlic powder, onion powder, dried thyme, dried oregano, and cayenne pepper to make a dry rub.
- Rub the dry spice mixture all over the pork shoulder, covering it evenly. Let it sit at room temperature for about 30 minutes to allow the flavors to penetrate the meat.

Slow Cook the Pork:
- Preheat your oven to 325°F (160°C).
- Place the seasoned pork shoulder in a roasting pan or Dutch oven.
- Pour the chicken or vegetable broth around the pork.
- Cover the pan tightly with foil or a lid.

- Roast the pork in the preheated oven for about 3-4 hours, or until the meat is very tender and can easily be pulled apart with a fork.

Shred the Pork:
- Remove the cooked pork shoulder from the oven.
- Transfer the pork to a cutting board and use two forks to shred the meat into bite-sized pieces, discarding any excess fat.

Add Barbecue Sauce:
- Place the shredded pork back into the roasting pan or a large bowl.
- Pour the barbecue sauce over the shredded pork and mix well to coat the meat evenly.

Assemble the Sandwiches:
- Toast the hamburger buns or sandwich rolls, if desired.
- Spoon a generous amount of pulled pork onto the bottom half of each bun.
- Top with coleslaw and pickles, if using.
- Place the top half of the bun over the filling to complete the sandwiches.

Serve and Enjoy:
- Serve the pulled pork sandwiches immediately while warm.
- Serve extra barbecue sauce on the side for dipping or drizzling over the sandwiches.

These pulled pork sandwiches are sure to be a hit at your summer feast. The tender and flavorful pork combined with the sweet and tangy barbecue sauce makes for a satisfying meal. Serve with your favorite sides like coleslaw, potato salad, or corn on the cob for a complete summer spread. Enjoy! Adjust the seasoning and spice levels according to your taste preferences.

Pesto Pasta Salad

Ingredients:

- 12 ounces (about 340g) pasta of your choice (such as fusilli, penne, or bowtie)
- 1 cup cherry tomatoes, halved
- 1/2 cup diced cucumber
- 1/4 cup sliced black olives
- 1/4 cup diced red onion
- 1/3 cup crumbled feta cheese (optional)
- 1/3 cup pine nuts, toasted (optional, for garnish)
- Fresh basil leaves, chopped (for garnish)

For the Pesto:

- 2 cups fresh basil leaves, packed
- 1/2 cup grated Parmesan cheese
- 1/3 cup pine nuts or walnuts
- 2 garlic cloves, peeled
- 1/2 cup extra virgin olive oil
- Salt and pepper, to taste

Instructions:

Cook the Pasta:
- Bring a large pot of salted water to a boil. Cook the pasta according to package instructions until al dente. Drain and rinse the pasta under cold water to stop the cooking process. Transfer the pasta to a large mixing bowl.

Make the Pesto:
- In a food processor, combine the fresh basil leaves, grated Parmesan cheese, pine nuts or walnuts, and garlic cloves. Pulse until finely chopped.
- With the food processor running, gradually add the olive oil in a steady stream until the pesto is smooth and well combined. Season with salt and pepper to taste.

Assemble the Pasta Salad:
- Add the cherry tomatoes, diced cucumber, sliced black olives, diced red onion, and crumbled feta cheese (if using) to the bowl with the cooked pasta.
- Pour the prepared pesto over the pasta and vegetables.

- Toss everything together until the pasta and vegetables are coated evenly with the pesto.

Chill and Serve:
- Cover the pesto pasta salad and refrigerate for at least 1 hour to allow the flavors to meld together.
- Before serving, give the salad a final toss.
- Garnish the salad with toasted pine nuts and chopped fresh basil leaves.

Enjoy!
- Serve the pesto pasta salad chilled as a delicious side dish or light main course.
- This salad is perfect for summer picnics, barbecues, or potlucks.

This pesto pasta salad is bursting with fresh flavors and can be customized with additional vegetables or protein (such as grilled chicken or shrimp) based on your preference. It's a versatile and crowd-pleasing dish that's sure to be a hit at any summer feast. Enjoy your homemade pesto pasta salad! Adjust the amount of pesto according to your taste preference for a more or less intense basil flavor.

Teriyaki Beef Kebabs

Ingredients:

- 1 ½ pounds (680g) beef sirloin or flank steak, cut into 1-inch cubes
- 1 red bell pepper, cut into chunks
- 1 green bell pepper, cut into chunks
- 1 red onion, cut into chunks
- 8-10 wooden or metal skewers

For the Teriyaki Marinade:

- 1/2 cup soy sauce
- 1/4 cup mirin (Japanese sweet rice wine)
- 1/4 cup honey or brown sugar
- 2 tablespoons rice vinegar
- 2 garlic cloves, minced
- 1-inch piece of ginger, grated
- 2 tablespoons sesame oil
- 2 tablespoons cornstarch (optional, for thickening)

Instructions:

    Prepare the Teriyaki Marinade:
- In a bowl, whisk together soy sauce, mirin, honey or brown sugar, rice vinegar, minced garlic, grated ginger, and sesame oil until well combined.
- Optional: To thicken the marinade for basting, stir in cornstarch until dissolved.

    Marinate the Beef:
- Place the beef cubes in a shallow dish or resealable plastic bag.
- Pour half of the teriyaki marinade over the beef, reserving the remaining marinade for basting.
- Toss the beef to coat evenly in the marinade.
- Cover the dish or seal the bag and refrigerate for at least 1 hour (or up to 4 hours) to allow the flavors to infuse.

    Prepare the Kebabs:
- If using wooden skewers, soak them in water for at least 30 minutes to prevent burning during grilling.
- Preheat your grill to medium-high heat.

    Assemble the Kebabs:

- Thread the marinated beef cubes onto the skewers, alternating with chunks of red bell pepper, green bell pepper, and red onion.

Grill the Kebabs:
- Place the assembled kebabs on the preheated grill.
- Cook for about 8-10 minutes, turning occasionally, or until the beef is cooked to your desired doneness and the vegetables are tender and slightly charred.

Baste with Marinade:
- During the last few minutes of grilling, brush the kebabs with the reserved teriyaki marinade for extra flavor and caramelization.

Serve:
- Remove the grilled teriyaki beef kebabs from the grill and transfer them to a serving platter.
- Serve the kebabs immediately while hot.
- Garnish with chopped green onions or sesame seeds, if desired.

Enjoy these delicious teriyaki beef kebabs as a main dish at your summer feast. They pair perfectly with steamed rice, noodles, or a fresh Asian-inspired salad. The tender, savory-sweet beef combined with the grilled vegetables and flavorful teriyaki marinade will be a hit with family and friends. Happy grilling! Adjust the cooking time based on the desired doneness of the beef cubes.

Gazpacho

Ingredients:

- 6 ripe tomatoes, chopped
- 1 cucumber, peeled and chopped
- 1 red bell pepper, seeded and chopped
- 1 small red onion, chopped
- 2 cloves garlic, minced
- 3 cups tomato juice or vegetable broth
- 1/4 cup extra virgin olive oil
- 2 tablespoons red wine vinegar or sherry vinegar
- 1 tablespoon lemon juice
- 1 teaspoon salt, or to taste
- 1/2 teaspoon black pepper
- 1/2 teaspoon ground cumin (optional)
- Dash of hot sauce (optional)
- Fresh basil or parsley, chopped (for garnish)

Instructions:

Prepare the Vegetables:
- In a large bowl, combine the chopped tomatoes, cucumber, red bell pepper, red onion, and minced garlic.

Blend the Soup:
- Transfer half of the chopped vegetables to a blender or food processor.
- Add half of the tomato juice or vegetable broth, olive oil, red wine vinegar, lemon juice, salt, black pepper, and ground cumin (if using).
- Blend until smooth and well combined.
- Pour the blended mixture into a large bowl.
- Repeat with the remaining chopped vegetables and liquid ingredients.

Adjust Seasoning:
- Taste the gazpacho and adjust the seasoning as needed. Add more salt, pepper, vinegar, or hot sauce according to your preference.

Chill the Gazpacho:
- Cover the bowl of gazpacho and refrigerate for at least 2 hours, or until well chilled.

Serve:
- Stir the gazpacho before serving to blend any separated ingredients.
- Ladle the chilled gazpacho into bowls or glasses.

- Garnish with chopped fresh basil or parsley.

Enjoy!

- Serve the gazpacho as a refreshing appetizer or light meal at your summer feast.
- You can also serve gazpacho with additional toppings such as diced avocado, croutons, or a drizzle of olive oil.

Gazpacho is best served cold and can be made ahead of time, making it a convenient dish for entertaining. It's a healthy and flavorful way to enjoy the abundance of summer vegetables. Customize the gazpacho by adjusting the amount of garlic, vinegar, or spices according to your taste preferences. Enjoy this delicious chilled soup at your summer feast!

Grilled Portobello Mushrooms

Ingredients:

- 4 large portobello mushrooms, stems removed
- 3 tablespoons balsamic vinegar
- 2 tablespoons soy sauce or tamari (for gluten-free)
- 2 tablespoons olive oil
- 2 garlic cloves, minced
- 1 teaspoon dried thyme
- Salt and black pepper, to taste
- Optional: Fresh herbs (such as parsley or rosemary) for garnish

Instructions:

Prepare the Marinade:
- In a small bowl, whisk together the balsamic vinegar, soy sauce or tamari, olive oil, minced garlic, dried thyme, salt, and black pepper.

Marinate the Portobello Mushrooms:
- Place the portobello mushrooms in a shallow dish or large resealable bag.
- Pour the marinade over the mushrooms, making sure they are well coated.
- Let the mushrooms marinate for at least 30 minutes, turning them occasionally to ensure even marination.

Preheat the Grill:
- Preheat an outdoor grill or grill pan over medium heat.

Grill the Portobello Mushrooms:
- Remove the marinated mushrooms from the dish or bag, reserving any excess marinade.
- Place the mushrooms on the preheated grill, gill-side down.
- Grill for about 4-5 minutes on each side, or until the mushrooms are tender and slightly charred, basting occasionally with the reserved marinade.

Serve:
- Remove the grilled portobello mushrooms from the grill and transfer them to a serving platter.
- Optionally, garnish with fresh herbs like parsley or rosemary.

Enjoy!
- Serve the grilled portobello mushrooms as a side dish or appetizer.
- You can also serve them as a vegetarian main course, perhaps on a bed of quinoa or couscous.

- These mushrooms are delicious on their own or served alongside grilled vegetables or a fresh salad.

Grilled portobello mushrooms are packed with savory flavors and have a meaty texture that makes them a satisfying option for vegetarians and mushroom lovers alike. They can be enjoyed hot off the grill or served at room temperature. Feel free to customize the marinade by adding your favorite herbs or spices. Enjoy these delicious grilled portobello mushrooms at your next summer feast!

Pineapple Chicken Kabobs

Ingredients:

- 1 ½ pounds boneless, skinless chicken breasts, cut into 1-inch cubes
- 1 fresh pineapple, peeled, cored, and cut into chunks
- 1 red bell pepper, cut into chunks
- 1 green bell pepper, cut into chunks
- 1 red onion, cut into chunks
- Wooden or metal skewers (if using wooden skewers, soak them in water for 30 minutes before grilling)

For the Marinade:

- 1/4 cup soy sauce
- 1/4 cup pineapple juice
- 2 tablespoons honey
- 2 tablespoons olive oil
- 2 garlic cloves, minced
- 1 teaspoon grated fresh ginger
- 1 tablespoon chopped fresh cilantro (optional)
- Salt and black pepper, to taste

Instructions:

Prepare the Marinade:
- In a bowl, whisk together soy sauce, pineapple juice, honey, olive oil, minced garlic, grated ginger, chopped cilantro (if using), salt, and black pepper.

Marinate the Chicken:
- Place the chicken cubes in a shallow dish or resealable bag.
- Pour the marinade over the chicken, making sure all pieces are well coated.
- Cover the dish or seal the bag and refrigerate for at least 1 hour (or up to 4 hours) to marinate.

Assemble the Kabobs:
- Preheat your grill to medium-high heat.
- Thread the marinated chicken cubes, pineapple chunks, red bell pepper chunks, green bell pepper chunks, and red onion chunks onto the skewers, alternating the ingredients.

Grill the Kabobs:
- Place the assembled kabobs on the preheated grill.
- Grill for about 10-12 minutes, turning occasionally, or until the chicken is cooked through and the vegetables are tender and slightly charred.

Serve:
- Remove the grilled pineapple chicken kabobs from the grill and transfer them to a serving platter.

Enjoy!
- Serve the pineapple chicken kabobs hot off the grill.
- Garnish with additional chopped cilantro, if desired.
- These kabobs can be served with rice, quinoa, or a fresh salad for a complete meal.

Pineapple chicken kabobs are bursting with sweet and savory flavors, making them a hit at any summer feast or barbecue. The marinade infuses the chicken with tropical notes from pineapple and ginger, complemented by the smoky char from grilling. Enjoy these delicious kabobs with family and friends! Adjust the seasoning and sweetness of the marinade according to your taste preferences.

Cucumber Mint Salad

Ingredients:

- 2 English cucumbers, thinly sliced
- 1/4 cup red onion, thinly sliced (optional)
- 2 tablespoons fresh mint leaves, finely chopped
- 2 tablespoons fresh dill, finely chopped (optional)
- 1/4 cup apple cider vinegar or white wine vinegar
- 2 tablespoons olive oil
- 1 tablespoon honey or maple syrup
- Salt and black pepper, to taste

Instructions:

Prepare the Cucumbers and Herbs:
- Wash the English cucumbers and slice them thinly using a mandoline or a sharp knife.
- Thinly slice the red onion, if using.
- Finely chop the fresh mint leaves and dill.

Assemble the Salad:
- In a large bowl, combine the sliced cucumbers, sliced red onion (if using), chopped mint leaves, and chopped dill.

Make the Dressing:
- In a small bowl, whisk together the apple cider vinegar or white wine vinegar, olive oil, honey or maple syrup, salt, and black pepper until well combined.

Toss the Salad:
- Pour the dressing over the cucumber mixture in the bowl.
- Toss everything together until the cucumbers and herbs are evenly coated with the dressing.

Chill and Serve:
- Cover the bowl with plastic wrap or a lid and refrigerate the cucumber mint salad for at least 30 minutes to allow the flavors to meld together.

Enjoy!
- Serve the cucumber mint salad chilled as a refreshing side dish.
- This salad pairs well with grilled meats, seafood, or as part of a mezze platter.

Cucumber mint salad is light, crisp, and bursting with fresh flavors. The combination of cool cucumbers, aromatic mint, and tangy dressing makes it a perfect addition to any summer meal. Feel free to customize this salad by adding cherry tomatoes, feta cheese, or olives for extra texture and flavor. Enjoy this delicious and healthy salad at your next summer feast! Adjust the sweetness and acidity of the dressing according to your taste preferences.

Fish Tacos with Chipotle Crema

Ingredients:

For the Fish Tacos:

- 1 pound white fish fillets (such as tilapia, cod, or mahi-mahi)
- 2 tablespoons olive oil
- 1 teaspoon chili powder
- 1/2 teaspoon ground cumin
- 1/2 teaspoon garlic powder
- Salt and black pepper, to taste
- 8-10 small flour or corn tortillas
- Shredded cabbage or lettuce, for serving
- Chopped fresh cilantro, for serving
- Lime wedges, for serving

For the Chipotle Crema:

- 1/2 cup sour cream or Greek yogurt
- 1-2 chipotle peppers in adobo sauce (canned), finely chopped
- 1 tablespoon adobo sauce (from the canned chipotle peppers)
- 1 tablespoon lime juice
- Salt, to taste

Instructions:

Prepare the Chipotle Crema:
- In a small bowl, whisk together the sour cream or Greek yogurt, finely chopped chipotle peppers, adobo sauce, lime juice, and a pinch of salt.
- Taste and adjust seasoning, adding more chipotle peppers or salt if desired. Set aside.

Prepare the Fish:
- Pat dry the fish fillets with paper towels.
- In a small bowl, mix together olive oil, chili powder, ground cumin, garlic powder, salt, and black pepper.
- Rub the spice mixture all over the fish fillets, coating them evenly.

Cook the Fish:
- Heat a grill pan or skillet over medium-high heat.

- Add the seasoned fish fillets to the pan and cook for 3-4 minutes per side, or until the fish is cooked through and flakes easily with a fork.
- Remove the cooked fish from the pan and let it rest for a few minutes.

Assemble the Tacos:
- Warm the tortillas on a skillet or in the microwave until soft and pliable.
- Divide the shredded cabbage or lettuce among the tortillas.
- Flake the cooked fish into chunks and distribute evenly among the tortillas.

Add Toppings:
- Drizzle each taco with chipotle crema.
- Sprinkle chopped fresh cilantro over the tacos.
- Serve with lime wedges on the side.

Enjoy!
- Serve the fish tacos with chipotle crema immediately.
- Enjoy these delicious tacos as a main course at your summer feast, accompanied by your favorite sides like rice and beans, or a fresh salad.

These fish tacos with chipotle crema are bursting with flavor and have the perfect balance of smoky, spicy, and creamy elements. They are easy to prepare and guaranteed to be a hit with family and friends. Customize the toppings to your liking by adding diced tomatoes, avocado slices, or pickled onions. Enjoy these irresistible fish tacos at your next summer gathering! Adjust the spiciness of the chipotle crema by adding more or less chipotle peppers according to your preference.

Tomato Basil Bruschetta

Ingredients:

- 4-5 ripe tomatoes, diced
- 1/2 cup fresh basil leaves, chopped
- 2 cloves garlic, minced
- 2 tablespoons extra virgin olive oil
- 1 tablespoon balsamic vinegar (optional)
- Salt and pepper, to taste
- Baguette or Italian bread, sliced
- Olive oil, for brushing bread

Instructions:

Prepare the Tomato Basil Mixture:
- In a medium bowl, combine the diced tomatoes, chopped fresh basil, minced garlic, extra virgin olive oil, and balsamic vinegar (if using).
- Season with salt and pepper to taste.
- Mix well to combine all the ingredients. Set aside to let the flavors meld together.

Prepare the Bread:
- Preheat the oven to 375°F (190°C).
- Slice the baguette or Italian bread into 1/2-inch thick slices.
- Place the bread slices on a baking sheet in a single layer.
- Lightly brush both sides of the bread slices with olive oil.

Toast the Bread:
- Place the baking sheet in the preheated oven and toast the bread slices for about 8-10 minutes, or until they are golden brown and crisp.
- Remove the toasted bread slices from the oven and let them cool slightly.

Assemble the Bruschetta:
- Spoon a generous amount of the tomato basil mixture onto each toasted bread slice.
- Drizzle any remaining juices from the tomato mixture over the bruschetta.

Serve:
- Arrange the tomato basil bruschetta on a platter.
- Garnish with additional chopped basil leaves, if desired.
- Serve immediately as a delightful appetizer at your summer feast.

Tomato basil bruschetta is best enjoyed fresh, with the flavors of ripe tomatoes and fragrant basil complementing each other perfectly. This appetizer is simple to prepare and showcases the vibrant tastes of summer. It's a crowd-pleasing dish that's sure to be a hit at any gathering. Serve alongside other appetizers or as part of a larger spread. Enjoy the delicious combination of flavors in this classic tomato basil bruschetta! Feel free to customize the recipe by adding diced onions, balsamic reduction, or a sprinkle of Parmesan cheese on top.

Grilled Vegetable Platter

Ingredients:

- Assorted vegetables of your choice, such as:
    - Zucchini, sliced lengthwise
    - Yellow squash, sliced lengthwise
    - Bell peppers (red, yellow, orange), halved or quartered
    - Eggplant, sliced into rounds
    - Red onions, sliced into thick rounds or wedges
    - Cherry tomatoes, kept whole
    - Asparagus spears
- Olive oil, for brushing
- Salt and black pepper, to taste
- Fresh herbs (such as parsley, basil, or thyme), chopped for garnish
- Balsamic glaze (optional), for drizzling

Instructions:

Prepare the Vegetables:
- Wash and dry all the vegetables.
- Slice the zucchini and yellow squash lengthwise into strips.
- Halve or quarter the bell peppers, removing the seeds and membranes.
- Slice the eggplant into rounds.
- Slice the red onions into thick rounds or wedges.
- Keep the cherry tomatoes and asparagus spears whole.

Preheat the Grill:
- Preheat an outdoor grill or grill pan over medium-high heat.

Grill the Vegetables:
- Lightly brush the vegetables with olive oil on both sides.
- Season with salt and black pepper to taste.
- Place the vegetables on the preheated grill, making sure not to overcrowd the grill.
- Grill the vegetables for a few minutes on each side, until they are tender and have grill marks.
- The cooking time will vary depending on the thickness of the vegetables. Cook until they are crisp-tender and lightly charred.

Assemble the Platter:
- Arrange the grilled vegetables on a large serving platter.

- Sprinkle chopped fresh herbs over the vegetables for added flavor and freshness.
- Optionally, drizzle with balsamic glaze for a sweet and tangy finish.

Serve:
- Serve the grilled vegetable platter warm or at room temperature.
- This dish can be served as a side dish, appetizer, or part of a vegetarian main course.
- Enjoy the vibrant flavors of grilled vegetables with friends and family at your summer feast!

Grilled vegetable platters are versatile and can be customized based on your favorite vegetables and seasonal produce. They are a healthy and delicious option for summer gatherings, adding color and variety to your table. Experiment with different vegetable combinations and serve alongside grilled meats, seafood, or as part of a Mediterranean-style meal. Enjoy the smoky-sweet flavors of grilled vegetables with this easy and satisfying dish! Adjust the seasoning and grilling time based on your preferences and the type of vegetables used.

Mango Coconut Rice

Ingredients:

- 1 cup jasmine rice (or any long-grain rice)
- 1 cup canned coconut milk
- 1 cup water
- 1 ripe mango, peeled, pitted, and diced
- 2 tablespoons sugar (adjust to taste)
- 1/4 teaspoon salt
- 1 teaspoon vanilla extract (optional)
- Toasted coconut flakes, for garnish (optional)
- Fresh mint leaves, for garnish (optional)

Instructions:

Prepare the Rice:
- Rinse the jasmine rice under cold water until the water runs clear.
- In a medium saucepan, combine the rinsed rice, coconut milk, water, sugar, and salt.
- If using vanilla extract, add it to the saucepan as well.
- Stir to combine.

Cook the Rice:
- Bring the mixture to a boil over medium-high heat.
- Reduce the heat to low, cover the saucepan with a tight-fitting lid, and simmer for 15-20 minutes, or until the rice is tender and all the liquid is absorbed.
- Remove the saucepan from the heat and let it sit, covered, for 5 minutes.

Add the Mango:
- While the rice is cooking, prepare the mango by peeling, pitting, and dicing it into small pieces.
- Once the rice is cooked and rested, gently fold in the diced mango pieces.

Serve:
- Transfer the mango coconut rice to a serving dish or individual bowls.
- Garnish with toasted coconut flakes and fresh mint leaves, if desired.

Enjoy!
- Serve the mango coconut rice warm as a side dish or dessert.
- This dish can be enjoyed on its own or paired with grilled seafood or chicken for a tropical-themed meal.

Mango coconut rice is creamy, fragrant, and naturally sweet from the mango and coconut milk. The combination of flavors and textures makes it a delightful addition to any summer feast or gathering. Feel free to adjust the sweetness by adding more or less sugar according to your taste preferences. Enjoy this delicious and exotic mango coconut rice with family and friends!

Lemon Garlic Shrimp Scampi

Ingredients:

- 1 pound large shrimp, peeled and deveined
- Salt and black pepper, to taste
- 4 tablespoons unsalted butter
- 4 cloves garlic, minced
- Zest of 1 lemon
- Juice of 1 lemon
- 1/4 cup dry white wine (or chicken broth)
- 1/4 teaspoon red pepper flakes (optional)
- 2 tablespoons chopped fresh parsley
- Cooked pasta or crusty bread, for serving

Instructions:

Prepare the Shrimp:
- Pat the shrimp dry with paper towels and season with salt and black pepper.

Cook the Shrimp:
- In a large skillet or pan, melt 2 tablespoons of butter over medium-high heat.
- Add the seasoned shrimp to the skillet in a single layer.
- Cook the shrimp for 1-2 minutes on each side, until they turn pink and opaque. Be careful not to overcook. Remove the shrimp from the skillet and set aside.

Make the Lemon Garlic Sauce:
- In the same skillet, add the remaining 2 tablespoons of butter.
- Add the minced garlic and cook for 1 minute until fragrant.
- Stir in the lemon zest, lemon juice, and white wine (or chicken broth).
- Add the red pepper flakes, if using, for a bit of heat.
- Let the sauce simmer for 2-3 minutes to reduce slightly.

Combine and Serve:
- Return the cooked shrimp to the skillet and toss with the lemon garlic sauce to coat evenly.
- Cook for an additional minute to heat the shrimp through.
- Sprinkle chopped fresh parsley over the shrimp scampi.

Serve:

- Serve the lemon garlic shrimp scampi immediately over cooked pasta or with crusty bread.
- Garnish with additional parsley and lemon wedges, if desired.

Enjoy!

- Enjoy this delicious lemon garlic shrimp scampi as a main course for dinner.
- The buttery lemon sauce complements the tender shrimp perfectly and is ideal for sopping up with pasta or bread.

This lemon garlic shrimp scampi is quick and easy to prepare, making it a great option for weeknight dinners or special occasions. The bright flavors of lemon and garlic pair beautifully with the shrimp, creating a dish that's both elegant and satisfying. Customize the dish by adjusting the amount of garlic, lemon, or red pepper flakes to suit your taste preferences. Bon appétit!

Avocado Corn Salad

Ingredients:

- 2 cups fresh or canned corn kernels (about 2 ears of corn)
- 2 ripe avocados, diced
- 1 cup cherry tomatoes, halved
- 1/4 cup red onion, finely chopped
- 1/4 cup fresh cilantro, chopped
- Juice of 2 limes
- 2 tablespoons extra virgin olive oil
- 1 clove garlic, minced
- Salt and pepper, to taste
- Optional: 1 jalapeño, seeded and diced (for a spicy kick)

Instructions:

Prepare the Corn:
- If using fresh corn, shuck the corn and remove the kernels using a knife.
- If using canned corn, drain and rinse the corn kernels.

Combine Ingredients:
- In a large bowl, combine the corn kernels, diced avocados, cherry tomatoes, chopped red onion, and chopped cilantro.
- If using jalapeño, add it to the bowl as well.

Make the Dressing:
- In a small bowl, whisk together the lime juice, extra virgin olive oil, minced garlic, salt, and pepper until well combined.

Assemble the Salad:
- Pour the dressing over the corn and avocado mixture.
- Gently toss everything together until the salad is evenly coated with the dressing.

Chill and Serve:
- Cover the bowl with plastic wrap or a lid and refrigerate the avocado corn salad for at least 30 minutes to allow the flavors to meld together.

Enjoy!
- Serve the avocado corn salad chilled as a refreshing side dish or appetizer.
- This salad pairs well with grilled chicken, fish, or as a topping for tacos.

Avocado corn salad is colorful, nutritious, and bursting with fresh flavors. The creamy avocado, sweet corn, and tangy lime dressing create a delightful combination that's sure to be a hit at any summer feast. Feel free to customize the salad by adding black beans, diced bell peppers, or crumbled feta cheese for extra texture and flavor. Enjoy this delicious avocado corn salad with family and friends! Adjust the seasoning and lime juice according to your taste preferences.

Hawaiian Pork Sliders

Ingredients:

For the Pork:

- 2 pounds pork shoulder or pork butt, trimmed of excess fat
- 1 cup pineapple juice
- 1/2 cup soy sauce
- 1/4 cup brown sugar
- 4 cloves garlic, minced
- 1 teaspoon ground ginger
- Slider buns, for serving

For the Pineapple Coleslaw:

- 2 cups shredded cabbage (green or purple)
- 1 cup diced pineapple (fresh or canned)
- 1/4 cup mayonnaise
- 1 tablespoon apple cider vinegar
- Salt and pepper, to taste

Instructions:

Prepare the Pork:
- In a slow cooker or crockpot, combine the pineapple juice, soy sauce, brown sugar, minced garlic, and ground ginger.
- Add the trimmed pork shoulder or pork butt to the slow cooker and coat it with the marinade.

Cook the Pork:
- Cover the slow cooker and cook on low heat for 6-8 hours, or until the pork is tender and easily shreds with a fork.
- Once cooked, shred the pork using two forks and mix it with the cooking juices in the slow cooker.

Prepare the Pineapple Coleslaw:
- In a large bowl, combine the shredded cabbage and diced pineapple.
- In a separate small bowl, whisk together the mayonnaise, apple cider vinegar, salt, and pepper to make the dressing.
- Pour the dressing over the cabbage and pineapple mixture and toss until well combined. Adjust seasoning to taste.

Assemble the Sliders:
- Slice the slider buns in half horizontally and lightly toast them, if desired.
- Place a generous portion of shredded Hawaiian pork on the bottom half of each slider bun.
- Top the pork with a spoonful of pineapple coleslaw.
- Place the top half of the slider bun over the coleslaw to assemble the sliders.

Serve:
- Arrange the Hawaiian pork sliders on a serving platter.
- Serve immediately and enjoy!

These Hawaiian pork sliders are sweet, savory, and packed with tropical flavors. The tender shredded pork combined with the tangy pineapple coleslaw makes for a delicious bite-sized sandwich that's perfect for any summer feast or party. Feel free to customize the sliders by adding barbecue sauce, sliced jalapeños, or additional toppings to suit your taste preferences. Serve these sliders with a side of potato chips, sweet potato fries, or a green salad for a complete meal. Enjoy these tasty Hawaiian pork sliders with friends and family! Adjust the sweetness and seasoning of the pork marinade to your liking.

Mediterranean Stuffed Bell Peppers

Ingredients:

- 4 large bell peppers (any color), tops cut off and seeds removed
- 1 cup cooked quinoa or rice (white or brown)
- 1 can (15 oz) chickpeas, drained and rinsed
- 1 cup diced tomatoes (canned or fresh)
- 1/2 cup diced cucumber
- 1/4 cup diced red onion
- 1/4 cup chopped Kalamata olives
- 2 tablespoons chopped fresh parsley
- 2 tablespoons chopped fresh mint
- 2 tablespoons olive oil
- 2 tablespoons lemon juice
- 2 cloves garlic, minced
- 1 teaspoon ground cumin
- Salt and black pepper, to taste
- Crumbled feta cheese, for garnish (optional)

Instructions:

Preheat the Oven:
- Preheat your oven to 375°F (190°C).

Prepare the Bell Peppers:
- Cut the tops off the bell peppers and remove the seeds and membranes from the inside. Set aside.

Prepare the Filling:
- In a large mixing bowl, combine the cooked quinoa or rice, chickpeas, diced tomatoes, diced cucumber, diced red onion, chopped Kalamata olives, chopped parsley, and chopped mint.

Make the Dressing:
- In a small bowl, whisk together the olive oil, lemon juice, minced garlic, ground cumin, salt, and black pepper.

Combine and Stuff the Peppers:
- Pour the dressing over the filling mixture in the large bowl.
- Toss everything together until well combined and evenly coated with the dressing.
- Spoon the filling mixture into the hollowed-out bell peppers, pressing down gently to pack the filling.

Bake the Stuffed Peppers:
- Place the stuffed bell peppers in a baking dish or on a baking sheet.
- Cover the dish with foil and bake in the preheated oven for 25-30 minutes, or until the peppers are tender and the filling is heated through.

Serve:
- Remove the foil from the baking dish and garnish the stuffed bell peppers with crumbled feta cheese, if desired.
- Serve the Mediterranean stuffed bell peppers hot as a delicious and satisfying main dish.

These Mediterranean stuffed bell peppers are colorful, flavorful, and packed with wholesome ingredients. They make a perfect vegetarian or vegan meal option and are great for entertaining guests. Feel free to customize the filling with your favorite Mediterranean-inspired ingredients, such as artichoke hearts, sun-dried tomatoes, or pine nuts. Enjoy these delicious stuffed bell peppers as a nutritious and satisfying dish at your next summer feast! Adjust the seasoning and herbs according to your taste preferences.

Grilled Eggplant with Tahini Sauce

Ingredients:

For the Grilled Eggplant:

- 2 medium-sized eggplants, sliced into 1/2-inch rounds
- Salt, for sprinkling
- Olive oil, for brushing

For the Tahini Sauce:

- 1/4 cup tahini (sesame paste)
- 2 tablespoons lemon juice
- 2 tablespoons water, or more as needed
- 1 clove garlic, minced
- Salt, to taste
- Chopped fresh parsley, for garnish (optional)
- Red pepper flakes, for garnish (optional)

Instructions:

Prepare the Eggplant:
- Place the eggplant slices on a paper towel-lined tray or cutting board.
- Sprinkle salt over both sides of the eggplant slices and let them sit for about 15-20 minutes. This helps draw out excess moisture and bitterness from the eggplant.

Preheat the Grill:
- Preheat an outdoor grill or grill pan over medium-high heat.

Grill the Eggplant:
- Pat the eggplant slices dry with paper towels to remove the moisture and salt.
- Brush both sides of the eggplant slices lightly with olive oil.
- Place the eggplant slices on the preheated grill and cook for about 3-4 minutes on each side, or until tender and grill marks appear. Cooking time may vary depending on the thickness of the slices.

Make the Tahini Sauce:
- In a small bowl, whisk together the tahini, lemon juice, minced garlic, and a pinch of salt.

- Gradually add water to the tahini mixture, whisking continuously, until you reach a smooth and pourable consistency. Add more water as needed to achieve the desired texture.

Assemble and Serve:
- Arrange the grilled eggplant slices on a serving platter.
- Drizzle the tahini sauce over the grilled eggplant slices.
- Garnish with chopped fresh parsley and red pepper flakes, if desired.

Enjoy!
- Serve the grilled eggplant with tahini sauce immediately as a delicious appetizer or side dish.
- This dish pairs well with pita bread, rice, or a fresh salad.

Grilled eggplant with tahini sauce is a wonderful way to enjoy the smoky flavor of grilled vegetables combined with the creamy richness of tahini. The tahini sauce adds a tangy and nutty flavor that complements the eggplant beautifully. This dish is not only delicious but also vegan-friendly and gluten-free. It's perfect for serving at barbecues, picnics, or as part of a Mediterranean-inspired meal. Enjoy this flavorful and healthy grilled eggplant dish with family and friends! Adjust the seasoning and lemon juice in the tahini sauce according to your taste preferences.

Berry Salad with Poppyseed Dressing

Ingredients:

For the Berry Salad:

- 6 cups mixed berries (such as strawberries, blueberries, raspberries, blackberries)
- 1 cup sliced fresh strawberries
- 1 cup sliced fresh kiwi (optional)
- 1/4 cup fresh mint leaves, chopped (optional)
- 1/4 cup sliced almonds or chopped pecans, toasted (optional)

For the Poppyseed Dressing:

- 1/3 cup mayonnaise
- 2 tablespoons honey or maple syrup
- 2 tablespoons apple cider vinegar
- 1 tablespoon lemon juice
- 1 tablespoon poppy seeds
- Pinch of salt

Instructions:

Prepare the Berry Salad:
- Rinse and gently dry the mixed berries.
- If using strawberries, hull and slice them.
- Slice the kiwi into rounds or halves, if using.
- In a large salad bowl, combine the mixed berries, sliced strawberries, sliced kiwi (if using), and chopped mint leaves. Toss gently to combine.

Prepare the Poppyseed Dressing:
- In a small bowl, whisk together the mayonnaise, honey or maple syrup, apple cider vinegar, lemon juice, poppy seeds, and a pinch of salt until well combined.

Assemble and Serve:
- Drizzle the poppyseed dressing over the mixed berries and gently toss to coat.
- Sprinkle the toasted sliced almonds or chopped pecans over the top of the salad.

Enjoy!

- Serve the berry salad with poppyseed dressing immediately as a refreshing side dish or dessert.
- This salad is perfect for summer gatherings, picnics, or as a light and healthy treat.

The combination of fresh berries, creamy poppyseed dressing, and crunchy nuts creates a delicious and colorful salad that's bursting with flavor. Feel free to customize the salad by using your favorite combination of berries and adding other fruits like sliced peaches or mandarin oranges. The poppyseed dressing adds a lovely sweetness and tanginess to the salad, making it a perfect complement to the fresh berries. Enjoy this delightful berry salad with poppyseed dressing with family and friends! Adjust the sweetness of the dressing by adding more or less honey or maple syrup according to your taste preferences.

Thai Peanut Noodles

Ingredients:

For the Peanut Sauce:

- 1/2 cup creamy peanut butter
- 1/4 cup soy sauce (or tamari for gluten-free)
- 2 tablespoons rice vinegar
- 2 tablespoons honey or maple syrup
- 2 cloves garlic, minced
- 1 tablespoon grated fresh ginger
- 1 tablespoon sesame oil
- 1 tablespoon sriracha or chili garlic sauce (adjust to taste)
- 1/4 cup warm water, or more as needed

For the Noodles:

- 12 oz (340g) rice noodles or linguine noodles
- 1 red bell pepper, thinly sliced
- 1 cucumber, julienned or thinly sliced
- 2 carrots, julienned or thinly sliced
- 1/4 cup chopped green onions (scallions)
- 1/4 cup chopped fresh cilantro
- 1/4 cup chopped roasted peanuts, for garnish
- Lime wedges, for serving

Instructions:

    Prepare the Peanut Sauce:
- In a bowl, whisk together the creamy peanut butter, soy sauce, rice vinegar, honey or maple syrup, minced garlic, grated ginger, sesame oil, and sriracha or chili garlic sauce until smooth.
- Gradually add warm water, a little at a time, and whisk until you reach a smooth and pourable consistency. Add more water if needed to thin out the sauce.

    Cook the Noodles:
- Cook the rice noodles or linguine noodles according to the package instructions until al dente. Drain and rinse under cold water to stop the cooking process. Set aside.

Assemble the Thai Peanut Noodles:
- In a large mixing bowl, combine the cooked and cooled noodles with the sliced red bell pepper, julienned cucumber, julienned carrots, chopped green onions, and chopped cilantro.
- Pour the prepared peanut sauce over the noodles and vegetables.
- Toss everything together until the noodles and vegetables are evenly coated with the peanut sauce.

Serve:
- Divide the Thai peanut noodles into serving bowls.
- Garnish with chopped roasted peanuts and additional cilantro.
- Serve with lime wedges on the side for squeezing over the noodles.

Enjoy!
- Serve the Thai peanut noodles as a main dish or side dish at your summer feast.
- This dish can be enjoyed warm, at room temperature, or chilled.
- Enjoy the creamy, savory, and slightly spicy flavors of these delicious Thai peanut noodles!

These Thai peanut noodles are packed with vibrant colors and bold flavors, making them a crowd-pleasing dish for any occasion. Feel free to customize the vegetables based on your preferences, adding broccoli florets, snap peas, or shredded cabbage. You can also add grilled chicken, tofu, or shrimp for a protein boost. This versatile dish is perfect for potlucks, picnics, or any summer gathering. Adjust the level of spiciness by adding more or less sriracha or chili garlic sauce according to your taste. Enjoy these flavorful Thai peanut noodles with friends and family!

Citrus Marinated Salmon

Ingredients:

- 4 salmon fillets (about 6 oz each), skin-on or skinless
- Zest of 1 lemon
- Zest of 1 orange
- Juice of 1 lemon
- Juice of 1 orange
- 2 tablespoons soy sauce (or tamari for gluten-free)
- 2 tablespoons honey or maple syrup
- 2 tablespoons olive oil
- 2 cloves garlic, minced
- 1 teaspoon grated fresh ginger
- Salt and black pepper, to taste
- Chopped fresh parsley or cilantro, for garnish (optional)
- Lemon or orange slices, for serving

Instructions:

Prepare the Marinade:
- In a bowl, whisk together the lemon zest, orange zest, lemon juice, orange juice, soy sauce, honey or maple syrup, olive oil, minced garlic, grated ginger, salt, and black pepper.

Marinate the Salmon:
- Place the salmon fillets in a shallow dish or a resealable plastic bag.
- Pour the marinade over the salmon, making sure to coat each fillet evenly.
- Cover the dish or seal the bag and refrigerate for at least 30 minutes, or up to 2 hours. For maximum flavor, marinate overnight if desired.

Cook the Salmon:
- Preheat your grill, oven, or skillet over medium-high heat.
- Grilling Method:
  - Preheat the grill to medium-high heat.
  - Remove the salmon from the marinade and discard the marinade.
  - Place the salmon fillets on the grill, skin-side down (if skin-on), and cook for about 4-5 minutes per side, or until the salmon is cooked to your desired doneness and has nice grill marks.
- Oven Method:
  - Preheat the oven to 400°F (200°C).
  - Line a baking sheet with parchment paper or foil.

- Place the salmon fillets on the prepared baking sheet.
- Bake for about 12-15 minutes, depending on the thickness of the fillets, or until the salmon is cooked through and flakes easily with a fork.
- Pan-Searing Method:
  - Heat a tablespoon of olive oil in a skillet over medium-high heat.
  - Remove the salmon from the marinade and pat dry with paper towels.
  - Place the salmon fillets in the hot skillet, skin-side down (if skin-on), and cook for about 3-4 minutes per side, or until golden brown and cooked through.

Serve:
- Transfer the cooked citrus-marinated salmon to a serving platter.
- Garnish with chopped fresh parsley or cilantro, if desired.
- Serve with lemon or orange slices on the side for squeezing over the salmon.

Enjoy!
- Serve the citrus-marinated salmon hot with your favorite side dishes, such as rice, roasted vegetables, or a fresh salad.
- This dish is perfect for summer gatherings and is sure to impress with its bright and zesty flavors.

Enjoy this delicious and healthy citrus-marinated salmon at your next summer feast! The combination of citrus, honey, and soy sauce creates a mouthwatering marinade that perfectly complements the rich flavor of the salmon. Feel free to customize the marinade by adding chili flakes for a spicy kick or fresh herbs like thyme or rosemary.

Caesar Salad with Grilled Chicken

Ingredients:

For the Grilled Chicken:

- 2 boneless, skinless chicken breasts
- Salt and black pepper, to taste
- 1 tablespoon olive oil
- 1 teaspoon dried Italian seasoning (optional)

For the Caesar Dressing:

- 1/2 cup mayonnaise
- 1/4 cup grated Parmesan cheese
- 2 tablespoons lemon juice
- 2 teaspoons Dijon mustard
- 2 cloves garlic, minced
- 1 teaspoon Worcestershire sauce
- Salt and black pepper, to taste

For the Caesar Salad:

- 1 large head of romaine lettuce, washed and chopped
- 1 cup croutons (store-bought or homemade)
- Additional grated Parmesan cheese, for garnish
- Lemon wedges, for serving

Instructions:

Prepare the Grilled Chicken:
- Season the chicken breasts with salt, black pepper, and dried Italian seasoning (if using).
- Heat olive oil in a grill pan or outdoor grill over medium-high heat.
- Grill the chicken breasts for 6-8 minutes per side, or until cooked through and internal temperature reaches 165°F (75°C). Remove from heat and let rest for a few minutes before slicing.

Make the Caesar Dressing:

- In a bowl, whisk together the mayonnaise, grated Parmesan cheese, lemon juice, Dijon mustard, minced garlic, Worcestershire sauce, salt, and black pepper until smooth and well combined. Adjust seasoning to taste.

Assemble the Caesar Salad:
- In a large salad bowl, add the chopped romaine lettuce.
- Pour the Caesar dressing over the lettuce and toss until the leaves are evenly coated with the dressing.
- Add the croutons to the salad and toss again to combine.

Slice the Grilled Chicken:
- Slice the grilled chicken breasts into thin strips or bite-sized pieces.

Serve:
- Divide the dressed Caesar salad among serving plates.
- Arrange the sliced grilled chicken on top of each salad.
- Garnish with additional grated Parmesan cheese.
- Serve immediately with lemon wedges on the side for squeezing over the salad.

Enjoy!
- Serve this delicious Caesar salad with grilled chicken as a main course for lunch or dinner.
- This salad pairs well with a side of garlic bread or a bowl of soup.

This Caesar salad with grilled chicken is a crowd-pleasing dish that's both flavorful and satisfying. The creamy homemade dressing, crisp romaine lettuce, and tender grilled chicken come together beautifully in each bite. Feel free to customize the salad by adding cherry tomatoes, sliced cucumbers, or bacon bits for extra flavor and texture. Enjoy this classic Caesar salad with grilled chicken at your next summer feast! Adjust the amount of dressing and seasoning according to your taste preferences.

Black Bean and Corn Salsa

Ingredients:

- 1 can (15 oz) black beans, drained and rinsed
- 1 cup corn kernels (fresh, frozen, or canned)
- 1 cup diced tomatoes (fresh or canned)
- 1/2 cup diced red onion
- 1/4 cup chopped fresh cilantro
- 1 jalapeño pepper, seeded and finely diced (optional)
- Juice of 2 limes
- 2 tablespoons olive oil
- 1 clove garlic, minced
- 1 teaspoon ground cumin
- Salt and pepper, to taste
- Tortilla chips, for serving

Instructions:

Prepare the Salsa:
- In a large mixing bowl, combine the black beans, corn kernels, diced tomatoes, diced red onion, chopped cilantro, and diced jalapeño pepper (if using).

Make the Dressing:
- In a small bowl, whisk together the lime juice, olive oil, minced garlic, ground cumin, salt, and pepper.

Combine and Chill:
- Pour the dressing over the black bean and corn mixture.
- Gently toss everything together until well combined and evenly coated with the dressing.
- Cover the bowl with plastic wrap or a lid and refrigerate for at least 30 minutes to allow the flavors to meld together.

Serve:
- Before serving, give the salsa a quick stir.
- Taste and adjust seasoning if needed with more salt, pepper, or lime juice.
- Transfer the black bean and corn salsa to a serving bowl or dish.

Enjoy!
- Serve the black bean and corn salsa with tortilla chips as a delicious appetizer or snack.
- This salsa also makes a great topping for tacos, grilled meats, or salads.

This black bean and corn salsa is bursting with fresh flavors and textures. The combination of sweet corn, hearty black beans, tangy tomatoes, and zesty lime dressing creates a delightful salsa that's perfect for summer gatherings, picnics, or parties. Feel free to customize the salsa by adding diced avocado, bell peppers, or mango for extra sweetness and crunch. Enjoy this flavorful black bean and corn salsa with tortilla chips or as a tasty accompaniment to your favorite dishes! Adjust the spiciness by adding more or less jalapeño pepper according to your taste preferences.

Spicy Grilled Sausages

Ingredients:

- 4 spicy Italian sausages (or your favorite spicy sausage variety)
- 2 tablespoons olive oil
- 1 tablespoon paprika
- 1 teaspoon garlic powder
- 1 teaspoon onion powder
- 1/2 teaspoon cayenne pepper (adjust to taste)
- Salt and black pepper, to taste
- Fresh parsley or cilantro, chopped (for garnish, optional)
- Lemon wedges, for serving

Instructions:

Preheat the Grill:
- Preheat an outdoor grill or grill pan over medium-high heat.

Prepare the Sausages:
- In a small bowl, mix together the olive oil, paprika, garlic powder, onion powder, cayenne pepper, salt, and black pepper to create a spice rub.
- Pat the sausages dry with paper towels.
- Rub the spice mixture all over the sausages, coating them evenly.

Grill the Sausages:
- Place the seasoned sausages on the preheated grill.
- Grill the sausages for about 12-15 minutes, turning occasionally, until they are cooked through and have nice grill marks on all sides.

Check for Doneness:
- Use a meat thermometer to check that the internal temperature of the sausages has reached 160°F (71°C).

Rest and Serve:
- Remove the grilled sausages from the grill and let them rest for a few minutes before serving.
- Optionally, garnish with chopped fresh parsley or cilantro for a pop of color and freshness.
- Serve the spicy grilled sausages hot with lemon wedges on the side for squeezing over the sausages.

Enjoy!
- Serve the spicy grilled sausages as a main dish with your favorite sides, such as potato salad, coleslaw, grilled vegetables, or crusty bread.

- These sausages are also great for slicing and serving in sandwiches or wraps.

Spicy grilled sausages are a fantastic addition to any summer feast, providing bold and zesty flavors that are sure to be a hit with your guests. Feel free to adjust the level of spiciness by adding more or less cayenne pepper to suit your taste preferences. Enjoy these delicious and easy-to-make spicy grilled sausages at your next gathering!

Ratatouille

Ingredients:

- 1 large eggplant, diced into 1-inch cubes
- 2 zucchinis, sliced into rounds
- 1 yellow bell pepper, diced
- 1 red bell pepper, diced
- 1 onion, diced
- 4 cloves garlic, minced
- 2 cups diced tomatoes (canned or fresh)
- 3 tablespoons tomato paste
- 2 tablespoons olive oil
- 1 teaspoon dried thyme
- 1 teaspoon dried oregano
- Salt and pepper, to taste
- Fresh basil leaves, chopped, for garnish

Instructions:

Prepare the Eggplant:
- Place the diced eggplant in a colander and sprinkle with salt. Let it sit for about 30 minutes to draw out excess moisture. Rinse the eggplant under cold water and pat dry with paper towels.

Sauté the Vegetables:
- In a large skillet or Dutch oven, heat olive oil over medium heat.
- Add the diced onion and bell peppers. Sauté for 5-7 minutes, until softened.

Add Garlic and Herbs:
- Add the minced garlic, dried thyme, and dried oregano to the skillet. Sauté for another minute until fragrant.

Cook the Eggplant and Zucchini:
- Add the diced eggplant and sliced zucchini to the skillet. Cook for about 5-7 minutes, stirring occasionally, until the vegetables start to soften.

Add Tomatoes and Tomato Paste:
- Stir in the diced tomatoes and tomato paste. Mix well to combine.

Simmer the Ratatouille:
- Reduce the heat to low and cover the skillet or Dutch oven.
- Let the ratatouille simmer for 20-25 minutes, stirring occasionally, until all the vegetables are tender and the flavors have melded together.

- If the ratatouille looks too dry, add a splash of water or vegetable broth.

Season and Garnish:
- Taste the ratatouille and season with salt and pepper to taste.
- Stir in chopped fresh basil leaves just before serving.

Serve:
- Serve the ratatouille hot, either as a vegetarian main dish or as a side dish.
- Ratatouille pairs well with crusty bread, rice, quinoa, or pasta.

Enjoy!
- Enjoy this delicious and colorful ratatouille with family and friends. It's a wonderful dish to celebrate the flavors of summer!

Ratatouille is a versatile dish that can be served warm or at room temperature. It's even better the next day as the flavors continue to develop. Feel free to customize this recipe by adding other seasonal vegetables like cherry tomatoes, mushrooms, or carrots. Ratatouille is not only delicious but also vegan, gluten-free, and packed with nutrients. Bon appétit!

Pesto Grilled Cheese

Ingredients:

- 4 slices of bread (your choice of bread, such as sourdough, ciabatta, or whole wheat)
- 4 tablespoons basil pesto (store-bought or homemade)
- 8 slices of cheese (such as mozzarella, provolone, cheddar, or Swiss)
- 2 tablespoons butter, softened

Instructions:

Prepare the Bread:
- Lay out the slices of bread on a clean surface.

Spread Pesto:
- Spread about 1 tablespoon of basil pesto evenly onto one side of each slice of bread.

Add Cheese:
- Place 2 slices of cheese on the pesto side of two bread slices. You can use a combination of different cheeses for extra flavor.

Assemble the Sandwiches:
- Place the remaining slices of bread on top of the cheese, pesto side down, to form sandwiches.

Grill the Sandwiches:
- Heat a large skillet or griddle over medium heat.
- Spread a little softened butter on the top side of each sandwich.

Cook the Sandwiches:
- Carefully place the sandwiches, buttered side down, onto the hot skillet or griddle.
- Cook for 3-4 minutes, or until the bottom side is golden brown and crispy.

Flip and Cook Again:
- Spread a little more softened butter on the top side of each sandwich.
- Use a spatula to carefully flip the sandwiches.
- Continue to cook for another 3-4 minutes, or until the second side is golden brown and the cheese is melted and gooey.

Serve:
- Remove the pesto grilled cheese sandwiches from the skillet or griddle.
- Cut each sandwich in half diagonally, if desired.
- Serve hot and enjoy!

Pesto grilled cheese sandwiches are perfect for a quick and satisfying lunch or dinner. The combination of savory basil pesto and melted cheese between crispy bread slices is simply irresistible. Serve these sandwiches with a side salad, tomato soup, or potato chips for a complete meal. Feel free to customize the recipe by adding sliced tomatoes, fresh spinach leaves, or cooked bacon to the sandwiches for extra flavor and texture. Enjoy these delicious pesto grilled cheese sandwiches with family and friends!

Melon Prosciutto Skewers

Ingredients:

- 1 ripe cantaloupe or honeydew melon
- 4 ounces (about 8 slices) of prosciutto, sliced thinly
- Fresh basil leaves (optional)
- Balsamic glaze, for drizzling (optional)
- Wooden skewers or toothpicks

Instructions:

Prepare the Melon:
- Cut the cantaloupe or honeydew melon into bite-sized cubes or balls using a melon baller or knife. Alternatively, you can cut the melon into small wedges.

Assemble the Skewers:
- Take a cube of melon and wrap it with a slice of prosciutto. If using basil leaves, add a small basil leaf between the melon and prosciutto.
- Thread the prosciutto-wrapped melon onto wooden skewers or toothpicks. Repeat until all the ingredients are used.

Arrange and Serve:
- Arrange the melon prosciutto skewers on a serving platter.
- If desired, drizzle with balsamic glaze for added flavor.

Enjoy!
- Serve the melon prosciutto skewers as a delicious and elegant appetizer at your summer feast.

These melon prosciutto skewers are perfect for entertaining and make a refreshing and flavorful starter. The combination of sweet melon, salty prosciutto, and aromatic basil (if using) creates a harmonious blend of flavors. The addition of balsamic glaze adds a touch of sweetness and acidity to complement the dish. Enjoy these tasty skewers with family and friends as a delightful appetizer or light snack!

Chicken Caesar Wraps

Ingredients:

- 2 boneless, skinless chicken breasts
- Salt and pepper, to taste
- Olive oil, for cooking
- 4 large flour tortillas (10-inch size)
- 2 cups chopped romaine lettuce
- 1/2 cup grated Parmesan cheese
- 1/2 cup Caesar dressing (store-bought or homemade)
- Optional additions: cherry tomatoes, sliced cucumbers, croutons

Instructions:

Cook the Chicken:
- Season the chicken breasts with salt and pepper on both sides.
- Heat a grill pan or skillet over medium-high heat and drizzle with olive oil.
- Cook the chicken breasts for about 6-8 minutes per side, or until fully cooked and nicely charred on the outside.
- Remove from heat and let the chicken rest for a few minutes before slicing into thin strips.

Prepare the Wraps:
- Lay out the flour tortillas on a clean work surface.

Assemble the Wraps:
- Spread a tablespoon of Caesar dressing onto each tortilla, leaving a border around the edges.
- Arrange chopped romaine lettuce on top of the dressing.
- Place sliced grilled chicken on top of the lettuce.
- Sprinkle grated Parmesan cheese over the chicken.

Add Optional Ingredients:
- If desired, add cherry tomatoes, sliced cucumbers, or croutons for extra flavor and texture.

Wrap the Tortillas:
- Fold in the sides of the tortilla over the filling, then roll up tightly from the bottom to enclose the filling.
- Secure the wraps with toothpicks if needed to hold them together.

Slice and Serve:
- Use a sharp knife to slice each wrap in half diagonally.
- Arrange the chicken Caesar wraps on a serving platter.

Enjoy!
- Serve the chicken Caesar wraps immediately, and enjoy them as a delicious and portable meal.
- These wraps are great for picnics, lunches, or quick dinners.

Feel free to customize these chicken Caesar wraps based on your preferences. You can use grilled shrimp or sliced deli chicken instead of grilled chicken breasts. You can also add additional ingredients such as avocado slices, bacon bits, or roasted red peppers for more flavor variations. These wraps are versatile, easy to make, and always a crowd-pleaser! Adjust the amount of Caesar dressing and Parmesan cheese according to your taste preferences. Enjoy your homemade chicken Caesar wraps!

Quinoa Tabbouleh

Ingredients:

- 1 cup quinoa, rinsed
- 2 cups water
- 1 pint cherry tomatoes, halved
- 1 English cucumber, diced
- 1 bunch fresh parsley, finely chopped
- 1/2 bunch fresh mint, finely chopped
- 3 green onions, thinly sliced
- Juice of 2-3 lemons
- 1/4 cup extra-virgin olive oil
- Salt and pepper, to taste

Instructions:

Cook the Quinoa:
- In a medium saucepan, combine the rinsed quinoa and water.
- Bring to a boil over medium-high heat, then reduce the heat to low.
- Cover and simmer for about 15-20 minutes, or until the quinoa is cooked and the water is absorbed.
- Remove from heat and let it sit, covered, for 5 minutes. Fluff the quinoa with a fork and let it cool completely.

Prepare the Vegetables and Herbs:
- While the quinoa is cooking, prepare the vegetables and herbs.
- Chop the cherry tomatoes, cucumber, parsley, mint, and green onions. Place them in a large mixing bowl.

Assemble the Tabbouleh:
- Add the cooked and cooled quinoa to the bowl of chopped vegetables and herbs.

Make the Dressing:
- In a small bowl, whisk together the lemon juice, olive oil, salt, and pepper to make the dressing.

Combine Everything:
- Pour the dressing over the quinoa and vegetable mixture.
- Toss everything together until well combined and evenly coated with the dressing.

Chill and Serve:

- Cover the bowl with plastic wrap or a lid and refrigerate for at least 1 hour to allow the flavors to meld together.

Enjoy!
- Serve the quinoa tabbouleh chilled as a side dish or a light main course.
- Garnish with additional fresh herbs or lemon wedges if desired.

Quinoa tabbouleh is a healthy and vibrant salad that's perfect for summer gatherings, potlucks, or meal prep. It's gluten-free, vegan, and packed with protein and nutrients from the quinoa and fresh vegetables. This dish can be enjoyed on its own or served alongside grilled meats, fish, or tofu. Feel free to customize the tabbouleh by adding diced bell peppers, olives, or feta cheese for additional flavor and texture. Enjoy this refreshing quinoa tabbouleh as a delicious and nutritious addition to your summer feast!

Teriyaki Salmon Burgers

Ingredients:

For the Salmon Patties:

- 1 pound fresh salmon fillets, skin removed
- 1/4 cup breadcrumbs (panko or regular)
- 1 egg
- 2 green onions, finely chopped
- 2 cloves garlic, minced
- 1 tablespoon soy sauce
- 1 tablespoon hoisin sauce
- 1 tablespoon sesame oil
- Salt and pepper, to taste
- Olive oil, for cooking

For the Teriyaki Glaze:

- 1/4 cup soy sauce
- 2 tablespoons honey or brown sugar
- 1 tablespoon rice vinegar
- 1 clove garlic, minced
- 1 teaspoon grated fresh ginger
- 1 tablespoon water
- 1 teaspoon cornstarch

For Serving:

- Burger buns
- Lettuce leaves
- Sliced tomatoes
- Sliced cucumbers
- Mayonnaise or aioli (optional)

Instructions:

Prepare the Teriyaki Glaze:
- In a small saucepan, combine the soy sauce, honey or brown sugar, rice vinegar, minced garlic, and grated ginger.

- In a separate small bowl, mix together the water and cornstarch until smooth. Add the cornstarch mixture to the saucepan.
- Bring the mixture to a simmer over medium heat, stirring constantly until the sauce thickens slightly.
- Remove from heat and set aside to cool.

Prepare the Salmon Patties:
- Pat dry the salmon fillets with paper towels, then chop them into small pieces.
- In a food processor, pulse the salmon until finely chopped (be careful not to over-process).
- Transfer the chopped salmon to a mixing bowl and add breadcrumbs, egg, chopped green onions, minced garlic, soy sauce, hoisin sauce, sesame oil, salt, and pepper.
- Mix until well combined. Form the mixture into 4-6 salmon patties, depending on the desired size.

Cook the Salmon Patties:
- Heat a drizzle of olive oil in a skillet over medium-high heat.
- Add the salmon patties to the skillet and cook for 3-4 minutes per side, or until golden brown and cooked through.

Assemble the Burgers:
- Toast the burger buns if desired.
- Spread mayonnaise or aioli on the bottom halves of the burger buns.
- Place a salmon patty on each bun bottom.
- Drizzle the teriyaki glaze over each salmon patty.
- Top with lettuce leaves, sliced tomatoes, and sliced cucumbers.
- Place the top halves of the burger buns on top.

Serve and Enjoy!
- Serve the teriyaki salmon burgers immediately, and enjoy the delicious flavors of sweet and savory teriyaki with juicy salmon patties.
- Serve with extra teriyaki glaze on the side for dipping or drizzling.

These teriyaki salmon burgers are a delightful and satisfying dish that's perfect for a summer feast or any occasion. They're packed with Asian-inspired flavors and can be customized with your favorite burger toppings. Enjoy these delicious burgers with family and friends!

Blueberry Crumble Bars

Ingredients:

For the Crust and Crumble Topping:

- 1 1/2 cups all-purpose flour
- 1/2 cup granulated sugar
- 1/2 teaspoon baking powder
- 1/4 teaspoon salt
- Zest of 1 lemon (optional)
- 1/2 cup (1 stick) unsalted butter, chilled and cut into small pieces
- 1 egg, lightly beaten
- 1 teaspoon vanilla extract
- 1 cup old-fashioned oats

For the Blueberry Filling:

- 3 cups fresh or frozen blueberries
- 1/3 cup granulated sugar
- 2 tablespoons cornstarch
- Juice of 1 lemon

Instructions:

  Preheat the Oven:
  - Preheat your oven to 350°F (175°C). Grease or line a 9x9-inch baking pan with parchment paper, leaving an overhang for easy removal.

  Make the Crust and Crumble Topping:
  - In a large mixing bowl, whisk together the flour, sugar, baking powder, salt, and lemon zest (if using).
  - Add the chilled butter pieces to the flour mixture. Using a pastry cutter or your fingers, work the butter into the flour mixture until it resembles coarse crumbs.
  - Add the beaten egg and vanilla extract to the mixture. Mix until the dough comes together.
  - Reserve about 1 cup of the mixture for the crumble topping.
  - Stir in the oats into the remaining dough mixture until combined.

  Prepare the Blueberry Filling:

- In a separate bowl, combine the blueberries, granulated sugar, cornstarch, and lemon juice. Gently toss until the blueberries are coated.

Assemble the Bars:
- Press the larger portion of the dough mixture into the bottom of the prepared baking pan to form an even crust.
- Spread the blueberry filling over the crust in an even layer.
- Sprinkle the reserved dough mixture (the crumble topping) evenly over the blueberry filling.

Bake the Bars:
- Place the baking pan in the preheated oven and bake for 40-45 minutes, or until the top is golden brown and the blueberry filling is bubbly.
- Remove from the oven and let the blueberry crumble bars cool completely in the pan on a wire rack.

Slice and Serve:
- Once cooled, use the parchment paper overhang to lift the bars out of the pan.
- Transfer the bars to a cutting board and slice into squares.

Enjoy!
- Serve the blueberry crumble bars as a delicious dessert or snack.
- Store any leftover bars in an airtight container at room temperature for up to 3 days, or refrigerate for longer storage.

These blueberry crumble bars are perfect for summer gatherings, picnics, or as a sweet treat to enjoy with a cup of coffee or tea. The combination of buttery crust, juicy blueberries, and crunchy oat topping is irresistible! Feel free to customize this recipe by using different berries or adding chopped nuts to the oat topping. Enjoy these delicious bars bursting with blueberry goodness!

Cornbread Muffins

Ingredients:

- 1 cup cornmeal (yellow or white)
- 1 cup all-purpose flour
- 1/4 cup granulated sugar
- 1 tablespoon baking powder
- 1/2 teaspoon salt
- 1 cup buttermilk (or substitute with milk + 1 tablespoon vinegar or lemon juice)
- 1/2 cup unsalted butter, melted and cooled slightly
- 2 large eggs

Optional Additions (choose one or more):

- 1/2 cup fresh or canned corn kernels (drained)
- 1/4 cup diced jalapeños or green chilies (for a spicy kick)
- 1/2 cup shredded cheddar cheese
- 2-3 slices cooked and crumbled bacon

Instructions:

Preheat the Oven:
- Preheat your oven to 375°F (190°C). Grease a 12-cup muffin tin or line with paper liners.

Mix Dry Ingredients:
- In a large mixing bowl, whisk together the cornmeal, flour, sugar, baking powder, and salt until well combined.

Combine Wet Ingredients:
- In a separate bowl, whisk together the buttermilk, melted butter, and eggs until smooth.

Combine Wet and Dry Ingredients:
- Pour the wet ingredients into the bowl of dry ingredients.
- Stir until just combined, being careful not to overmix. The batter will be slightly lumpy.

Add Optional Mix-Ins (if using):
- Gently fold in any optional additions such as corn kernels, diced jalapeños, shredded cheese, or crumbled bacon.

Fill Muffin Cups:

- Divide the batter evenly among the prepared muffin cups, filling each about 3/4 full.

Bake the Muffins:
- Place the muffin tin in the preheated oven.
- Bake for 15-18 minutes, or until the tops of the muffins are golden brown and a toothpick inserted into the center comes out clean.

Cool and Serve:
- Remove the muffin tin from the oven and let the cornbread muffins cool in the pan for 5 minutes.
- Transfer the muffins to a wire rack to cool completely or serve warm.

Enjoy!
- Serve the cornbread muffins alongside your favorite dishes such as chili, barbecue, soups, or enjoy them as a snack with butter or honey.

These homemade cornbread muffins are moist, tender, and full of flavor. They're perfect for any occasion and can be customized with your favorite mix-ins. Experiment with different additions to suit your taste preferences. Store leftover muffins in an airtight container at room temperature for up to 2 days or freeze for longer storage. Enjoy these delicious cornbread muffins as a versatile and tasty side dish!

Lemon Herb Grilled Zucchini

Ingredients:

- 2-3 medium zucchini, sliced lengthwise into 1/4-inch thick strips
- Zest and juice of 1-2 lemons
- 3 tablespoons extra-virgin olive oil
- 2 cloves garlic, minced
- 2 tablespoons chopped fresh herbs (such as basil, parsley, or thyme)
- Salt and black pepper, to taste

Instructions:

Prepare the Zucchini:
- Wash the zucchini and trim off the ends. Slice the zucchini lengthwise into 1/4-inch thick strips. You can also cut them into rounds if preferred.

Make the Marinade:
- In a small bowl, whisk together the lemon zest, lemon juice, olive oil, minced garlic, chopped fresh herbs, salt, and black pepper.

Marinate the Zucchini:
- Place the zucchini strips in a shallow dish or a large resealable plastic bag.
- Pour the marinade over the zucchini, making sure to coat each piece evenly.
- Allow the zucchini to marinate for at least 15-30 minutes at room temperature, or refrigerate for up to 2 hours to enhance the flavors.

Preheat the Grill:
- Preheat an outdoor grill or grill pan over medium-high heat.

Grill the Zucchini:
- Remove the zucchini from the marinade, shaking off any excess.
- Place the zucchini strips directly on the preheated grill.
- Grill for 3-4 minutes per side, or until the zucchini is tender and grill marks appear.
- Avoid moving the zucchini too much while grilling to get nice char marks.

Serve:
- Transfer the grilled zucchini to a serving platter.
- Drizzle any remaining marinade over the grilled zucchini for extra flavor.
- Garnish with additional fresh herbs if desired.

Enjoy!

- Serve the lemon herb grilled zucchini as a delicious side dish alongside grilled meats, fish, or as part of a vegetarian meal.
- These zucchini slices are also great in salads, pasta dishes, or sandwiches.

Lemon herb grilled zucchini is a perfect summer side dish that's bursting with fresh flavors. The combination of zesty lemon, aromatic herbs, and smoky grilled zucchini creates a delightful dish that will complement any meal. Feel free to customize the recipe by adding other vegetables or spices to suit your taste preferences. Enjoy this easy and healthy grilled zucchini recipe!

Watermelon Mint Cooler

Ingredients:

- 4 cups cubed seedless watermelon
- 1/4 cup fresh mint leaves, plus extra for garnish
- Juice of 1 lime
- 2 tablespoons honey or agave syrup (adjust to taste)
- 2 cups cold water
- Ice cubes, for serving

Instructions:

Prepare the Watermelon:
- Cut the seedless watermelon into small cubes, discarding any seeds.

Blend the Ingredients:
- In a blender, combine the cubed watermelon, fresh mint leaves, lime juice, and honey or agave syrup.
- Blend until smooth and well combined.

Strain (Optional):
- If desired, strain the watermelon mixture through a fine-mesh sieve or cheesecloth to remove any pulp. This step is optional depending on your preference for texture.

Add Cold Water:
- Pour the watermelon mixture into a pitcher.
- Add 2 cups of cold water and stir to combine.

Chill:
- Refrigerate the watermelon mint mixture for at least 30 minutes to chill.

Serve:
- Fill glasses with ice cubes.
- Pour the chilled watermelon mint cooler into the glasses.
- Garnish with extra mint leaves.

Enjoy!
- Serve immediately and enjoy this refreshing watermelon mint cooler on a hot day.

This watermelon mint cooler is a simple and healthy drink that's naturally sweetened with watermelon and flavored with fresh mint and lime. It's a great alternative to sugary beverages and can be easily customized by adjusting the sweetness or adding a splash of sparkling water for fizziness. Feel free to experiment with different variations by adding a dash of vodka or rum for an adult-friendly cocktail version. Sip and savor this delightful watermelon mint cooler to stay cool and hydrated all summer long!

Mediterranean Chickpea Salad

Ingredients:

- 2 cans (15 ounces each) chickpeas (garbanzo beans), drained and rinsed
- 1 cucumber, diced
- 1 bell pepper (red, yellow, or orange), diced
- 1 pint cherry tomatoes, halved
- 1/2 red onion, thinly sliced
- 1/4 cup Kalamata olives, pitted and halved
- 1/4 cup chopped fresh parsley
- 1/4 cup chopped fresh mint
- 1/3 cup crumbled feta cheese (optional)
- Juice of 1 lemon
- 3 tablespoons extra-virgin olive oil
- 1 tablespoon red wine vinegar
- 1 garlic clove, minced
- 1 teaspoon dried oregano
- Salt and pepper, to taste

Instructions:

Prepare the Chickpeas:
- Drain and rinse the chickpeas (garbanzo beans) under cold water. Transfer them to a large mixing bowl.

Chop the Vegetables:
- Dice the cucumber, bell pepper, and red onion. Halve the cherry tomatoes. Add them to the bowl with the chickpeas.

Add the Herbs and Olives:
- Chop the fresh parsley and mint. Add them to the bowl along with the halved Kalamata olives.

Make the Dressing:
- In a small bowl, whisk together the lemon juice, olive oil, red wine vinegar, minced garlic, dried oregano, salt, and pepper to make the dressing.

Combine Everything:
- Pour the dressing over the chickpea and vegetable mixture in the large bowl.
- Toss everything together until well combined and evenly coated with the dressing.

Add Optional Ingredients:

- If using crumbled feta cheese, sprinkle it over the salad and gently toss to incorporate.

Chill and Serve:
- Cover the bowl with plastic wrap or a lid and refrigerate the Mediterranean chickpea salad for at least 30 minutes to allow the flavors to meld together.

Enjoy!
- Serve the Mediterranean chickpea salad chilled as a side dish or a light meal.
- This salad is perfect for picnics, potlucks, or as a healthy lunch option.
- Garnish with additional fresh herbs or a wedge of lemon before serving, if desired.

This Mediterranean chickpea salad is packed with protein, fiber, and a variety of textures and flavors. It's a versatile dish that can be customized by adding or substituting different vegetables and herbs based on what you have on hand. Enjoy this delicious and nutritious salad as a taste of the Mediterranean!

Honey Lime Chicken Wings

Ingredients:

- 2 pounds chicken wings, split into wingettes and drumettes
- Salt and pepper, to taste
- 2 tablespoons olive oil or vegetable oil
- 1/4 cup honey
- Zest and juice of 2 limes
- 2 cloves garlic, minced
- 1 tablespoon soy sauce or tamari (gluten-free soy sauce)
- 1 tablespoon sriracha sauce (adjust to taste)
- Chopped fresh cilantro, for garnish (optional)
- Lime wedges, for serving

Instructions:

Preheat the Oven:
- Preheat your oven to 400°F (200°C). Line a baking sheet with aluminum foil and lightly grease with cooking spray or oil.

Season the Chicken Wings:
- Pat the chicken wings dry with paper towels and place them in a large mixing bowl.
- Season the wings with salt and pepper, to taste. Drizzle with olive oil or vegetable oil and toss to coat evenly.

Bake the Chicken Wings:
- Arrange the seasoned chicken wings in a single layer on the prepared baking sheet.
- Bake in the preheated oven for 40-45 minutes, flipping halfway through, or until the wings are golden brown and crispy.

Make the Honey Lime Glaze:
- While the chicken wings are baking, prepare the honey lime glaze.
- In a small saucepan, combine the honey, lime zest, lime juice, minced garlic, soy sauce, and sriracha sauce.
- Heat over medium heat, stirring occasionally, until the mixture starts to bubble. Reduce the heat to low and simmer for 2-3 minutes until slightly thickened.

Coat the Wings with Glaze:
- Once the chicken wings are cooked and crispy, remove them from the oven.

- Brush or drizzle the honey lime glaze over the hot wings, turning to coat evenly.

Serve:
- Transfer the glazed honey lime chicken wings to a serving platter.
- Garnish with chopped fresh cilantro, if desired.
- Serve immediately with lime wedges on the side for squeezing over the wings.

Enjoy!
- Enjoy these delicious honey lime chicken wings as a tasty appetizer or main dish.
- Serve with your favorite dipping sauce, such as ranch dressing or blue cheese dressing, and enjoy!

These honey lime chicken wings are sweet, tangy, and packed with flavor. They're sure to be a hit at your next gathering or family dinner. Feel free to adjust the amount of sriracha sauce to your desired level of spiciness. Serve these wings with a side of rice, coleslaw, or a fresh green salad for a complete meal. Enjoy!

Stuffed Jalapeños

Ingredients:

- 12 fresh jalapeño peppers
- 8 ounces cream cheese, softened
- 1 cup shredded cheddar cheese (or Monterey Jack cheese)
- 1/2 teaspoon garlic powder
- 1/2 teaspoon onion powder
- 1/2 teaspoon paprika
- Salt and black pepper, to taste
- Optional: Cooked and crumbled bacon, chopped fresh cilantro or green onions for garnish

Instructions:

Prepare the Jalapeños:
- Preheat your oven to 375°F (190°C). Line a baking sheet with parchment paper or aluminum foil for easy cleanup.
- Wash the jalapeño peppers and cut them in half lengthwise. Use a spoon to scoop out the seeds and membranes, creating little jalapeño boats. Wear gloves to protect your hands from the heat if desired.

Make the Cheese Filling:
- In a mixing bowl, combine the softened cream cheese, shredded cheddar cheese, garlic powder, onion powder, paprika, salt, and black pepper. Mix until smooth and well combined.
- Optionally, mix in cooked and crumbled bacon for added flavor.

Fill the Jalapeños:
- Spoon the cheese mixture into each jalapeño half, pressing gently to fill them evenly.

Bake the Stuffed Jalapeños:
- Arrange the stuffed jalapeños on the prepared baking sheet.
- Bake in the preheated oven for 15-20 minutes, or until the cheese is melted and bubbly, and the jalapeños are tender.
- For a golden brown topping, you can broil the stuffed jalapeños for an additional 1-2 minutes, watching carefully to avoid burning.

Serve:
- Remove the stuffed jalapeños from the oven and let them cool slightly.
- Garnish with chopped fresh cilantro, green onions, or additional toppings if desired.

- Serve warm as a delicious appetizer or snack.

Enjoy!
- Enjoy these cheesy and spicy stuffed jalapeños with friends and family.
- Serve them alongside sour cream, salsa, or guacamole for dipping.

These stuffed jalapeños are a crowd-pleaser and can be easily customized based on your preferences. Feel free to experiment with different types of cheese, spices, or fillings like ground sausage or diced veggies. Adjust the amount of jalapeños used based on your spice tolerance. Whether baked in the oven or grilled on the barbecue, these stuffed jalapeños are sure to be a hit at any gathering!

Grilled Flatbread with Hummus

Ingredients:

- 4 pieces of flatbread (such as pita bread or naan)
- 1 cup hummus (store-bought or homemade)
- 1 tablespoon olive oil
- 1 clove garlic, minced
- Salt and pepper, to taste
- Optional toppings: sliced cherry tomatoes, diced cucumbers, chopped red onion, crumbled feta cheese, fresh herbs (such as parsley or cilantro), drizzle of balsamic glaze

Instructions:

Preheat the Grill:
- Preheat your grill to medium-high heat.

Prepare the Flatbread:
- In a small bowl, combine the olive oil, minced garlic, salt, and pepper.
- Brush both sides of each piece of flatbread with the olive oil mixture.

Grill the Flatbread:
- Place the oiled flatbread directly on the grill grates.
- Grill for 2-3 minutes per side, or until the bread is lightly charred and crispy.
- Remove the grilled flatbread from the grill and let it cool slightly.

Assemble the Grilled Flatbread with Hummus:
- Spread a generous amount of hummus over each piece of grilled flatbread.
- Top the hummus with your favorite toppings, such as sliced cherry tomatoes, diced cucumbers, chopped red onion, crumbled feta cheese, and fresh herbs.

Serve and Enjoy:
- Cut the grilled flatbread into wedges or squares.
- Arrange the grilled flatbread with hummus on a serving platter.
- Drizzle with a little balsamic glaze for added flavor, if desired.

Serve Immediately:
- Serve the grilled flatbread with hummus immediately while still warm.
- Enjoy as a delicious appetizer, light meal, or snack.

This grilled flatbread with hummus is versatile and customizable, so feel free to use your favorite toppings and add-ons. You can also add grilled vegetables, olives, or roasted red peppers for extra flavor. This dish is perfect for entertaining or as a quick and easy meal option. Enjoy the combination of crispy grilled flatbread and creamy hummus in this tasty Mediterranean-inspired recipe!

Summer Berry Trifle

Ingredients:

- 1 store-bought pound cake or angel food cake, cut into cubes
- 4 cups mixed fresh berries (such as strawberries, blueberries, raspberries, blackberries)
- 1/4 cup sugar (adjust based on sweetness of berries)
- 1 tablespoon lemon juice
- 2 cups heavy cream
- 1/4 cup powdered sugar
- 1 teaspoon vanilla extract
- Optional: 1/4 cup berry liqueur (such as Chambord or Framboise)

Instructions:

Prepare the Berries:
- In a bowl, toss the mixed berries with sugar and lemon juice. Let them sit for about 15-20 minutes to macerate and release their juices.

Whip the Cream:
- In a separate bowl, whip the heavy cream with powdered sugar and vanilla extract until stiff peaks form. Set aside.

Assemble the Trifle:
- In a trifle dish or glass bowl, start by layering half of the cake cubes at the bottom.
- If using, drizzle the cake cubes with half of the berry liqueur for extra flavor (optional).
- Spoon half of the macerated berries over the cake layer, including some of the juices.
- Spread half of the whipped cream over the berries, smoothing it out evenly.

Repeat the Layers:
- Repeat the layers: remaining cake cubes, remaining berries (with juices), and remaining whipped cream.

Garnish:
- Garnish the top of the trifle with extra berries for decoration.

Chill and Serve:
- Cover the trifle with plastic wrap and refrigerate for at least 2-3 hours, or overnight, to allow the flavors to meld and the cake to absorb the juices.

Serve:

- Before serving, garnish with fresh mint leaves or additional berries, if desired.
- Scoop out servings of the summer berry trifle into individual dessert bowls or glasses.

Enjoy!
- Enjoy this refreshing and decadent summer berry trifle as a delightful dessert for any occasion.

This summer berry trifle is versatile, and you can customize it based on your preferences. Feel free to use different types of berries or substitute the pound cake with sponge cake or ladyfingers. You can also add a layer of lemon curd or pastry cream for extra richness. This dessert is perfect for summer gatherings, potlucks, or as a special treat to enjoy with family and friends. Indulge in the sweet and fruity flavors of this beautiful summer dessert!

BBQ Chicken Pizza

Ingredients:

- 1 pound pizza dough (homemade or store-bought)
- 1/2 cup barbecue sauce (your favorite kind)
- 2 cups cooked and shredded chicken (rotisserie chicken works well)
- 1 cup shredded mozzarella cheese
- 1/2 red onion, thinly sliced
- 1/4 cup chopped fresh cilantro (optional)
- Olive oil, for brushing
- Cornmeal or flour, for dusting

Instructions:

Preheat the Oven:
- Preheat your oven to the temperature recommended for your pizza dough (usually around 450°F or 230°C).

Prepare the Pizza Dough:
- If using store-bought pizza dough, follow the package instructions for bringing it to room temperature.
- On a lightly floured surface, roll out the pizza dough into a round or rectangular shape, about 1/4 inch thick.

Prepare the Pizza Toppings:
- In a bowl, toss the shredded chicken with a few tablespoons of barbecue sauce to coat.

Assemble the Pizza:
- Place the rolled-out pizza dough on a baking sheet or pizza stone that has been lightly dusted with cornmeal or flour to prevent sticking.
- Brush the edges of the dough with olive oil to create a golden crust.
- Spread the remaining barbecue sauce evenly over the pizza dough, leaving a small border around the edges.
- Sprinkle half of the shredded mozzarella cheese over the barbecue sauce.
- Distribute the barbecue chicken and sliced red onion evenly over the cheese.

Add Remaining Toppings:
- Sprinkle the remaining shredded mozzarella cheese over the top of the pizza.

Bake the Pizza:
- Transfer the assembled pizza into the preheated oven.

- Bake for 12-15 minutes, or until the crust is golden brown and the cheese is melted and bubbly.

Garnish and Serve:
- Remove the BBQ chicken pizza from the oven.
- Sprinkle chopped fresh cilantro over the hot pizza, if desired, for a pop of freshness and flavor.

Slice and Enjoy:
- Let the pizza cool slightly before slicing into wedges or squares.
- Serve hot and enjoy your homemade BBQ chicken pizza!

Feel free to customize this BBQ chicken pizza with additional toppings such as sliced bell peppers, jalapeños, or cooked bacon. You can also use a blend of cheeses like cheddar, gouda, or smoked mozzarella for added depth of flavor. This pizza is perfect for casual dinners, game nights, or any occasion where you want to enjoy a delicious and satisfying meal. Enjoy the savory and tangy flavors of BBQ chicken pizza straight from your own kitchen!

Key Lime Pie

Ingredients:

For the Graham Cracker Crust:

- 1 1/2 cups graham cracker crumbs (about 10-12 graham crackers)
- 1/4 cup granulated sugar
- 6 tablespoons unsalted butter, melted

For the Key Lime Filling:

- 1 can (14 ounces) sweetened condensed milk
- 4 large egg yolks
- 1/2 cup freshly squeezed key lime juice (or regular lime juice)
- Zest of 1 lime (optional)

For the Whipped Cream Topping:

- 1 cup heavy cream
- 2 tablespoons powdered sugar
- 1/2 teaspoon vanilla extract

Instructions:

Preheat the Oven:
- Preheat your oven to 350°F (175°C).

Make the Graham Cracker Crust:
- In a mixing bowl, combine the graham cracker crumbs, granulated sugar, and melted butter. Stir until the mixture resembles wet sand.
- Press the crumb mixture evenly into the bottom and up the sides of a 9-inch pie dish.
- Use the bottom of a measuring cup or glass to firmly pack the crust.
- Bake the crust in the preheated oven for 10 minutes. Remove from the oven and let it cool slightly.

Prepare the Key Lime Filling:
- In a separate mixing bowl, whisk together the sweetened condensed milk, egg yolks, key lime juice, and lime zest (if using) until smooth and well combined.
- Pour the filling into the partially baked graham cracker crust.

Bake the Pie:
- Return the pie to the oven and bake for 15-18 minutes, or until the filling is set but still slightly jiggly in the center.
- Remove the pie from the oven and let it cool completely on a wire rack. Refrigerate for at least 2 hours or until well chilled.

Make the Whipped Cream Topping:
- In a chilled mixing bowl, whip the heavy cream, powdered sugar, and vanilla extract until stiff peaks form.

Serve the Key Lime Pie:
- Spread or pipe the whipped cream over the chilled key lime pie.
- Optionally, garnish with additional lime zest or slices before serving.

Enjoy!
- Slice and serve the key lime pie chilled.
- Store any leftovers covered in the refrigerator for up to 3 days.

Key lime pie is a refreshing and delightful dessert that's perfect for summer gatherings or any occasion. The combination of tart lime filling with a sweet graham cracker crust is simply irresistible. Enjoy this homemade key lime pie with friends and family, and savor the bright flavors of this classic dessert!

Peach Cobbler

Ingredients:

For the Peach Filling:

- 6-8 ripe peaches, peeled, pitted, and sliced (about 6 cups)
- 1/2 cup granulated sugar
- 2 tablespoons all-purpose flour
- 1 teaspoon ground cinnamon
- 1/4 teaspoon ground nutmeg
- 1 tablespoon fresh lemon juice

For the Biscuit Topping:

- 1 cup all-purpose flour
- 1/2 cup granulated sugar
- 1 teaspoon baking powder
- 1/4 teaspoon salt
- 1/2 cup unsalted butter, melted
- 1/4 cup boiling water

For Serving:

- Vanilla ice cream or whipped cream (optional)

Instructions:

Preheat the Oven:
- Preheat your oven to 375°F (190°C).

Prepare the Peach Filling:
- In a large mixing bowl, combine the sliced peaches, granulated sugar, flour, cinnamon, nutmeg, and lemon juice.
- Toss the mixture gently until the peaches are well coated. Set aside while you prepare the biscuit topping.

Make the Biscuit Topping:
- In another mixing bowl, whisk together the flour, sugar, baking powder, and salt.
- Add the melted butter and stir until the mixture resembles coarse crumbs.

- Gradually add the boiling water to the biscuit mixture, stirring until just combined. The dough will be thick and sticky.

Assemble the Peach Cobbler:
- Transfer the peach filling into a 9x13-inch baking dish or a similar-sized casserole dish.
- Drop spoonfuls of the biscuit dough evenly over the top of the peach mixture. Use a spatula or back of a spoon to spread the dough slightly, but it's okay if some peach filling peeks through.

Bake the Cobbler:
- Place the baking dish in the preheated oven and bake for 40-45 minutes, or until the topping is golden brown and the peach filling is bubbly.

Serve Warm:
- Remove the peach cobbler from the oven and let it cool slightly before serving.
- Serve warm with a scoop of vanilla ice cream or a dollop of whipped cream, if desired.

Enjoy!
- Enjoy this homemade peach cobbler as a delightful summer dessert.
- Store any leftovers covered in the refrigerator and reheat before serving.

This peach cobbler recipe is easy to make and perfect for using fresh, ripe peaches when they're in season. The combination of tender peaches and buttery biscuit topping is absolutely delicious. Serve it warm and enjoy the comforting flavors of this classic Southern dessert!

Strawberry Shortcake

Ingredients:

For the Shortcake Biscuits:

- 2 cups all-purpose flour
- 1/4 cup granulated sugar
- 1 tablespoon baking powder
- 1/2 teaspoon salt
- 1/2 cup cold unsalted butter, cut into small pieces
- 3/4 cup heavy cream
- 1 teaspoon vanilla extract

For the Strawberry Filling:

- 1 1/2 pounds fresh strawberries, hulled and sliced
- 1/4 cup granulated sugar (adjust based on sweetness of strawberries)
- 1 teaspoon lemon juice

For the Whipped Cream:

- 1 cup heavy cream, chilled
- 2 tablespoons powdered sugar
- 1 teaspoon vanilla extract

Instructions:

Prepare the Shortcake Biscuits:
- Preheat your oven to 400°F (200°C). Line a baking sheet with parchment paper.
- In a large mixing bowl, whisk together the flour, sugar, baking powder, and salt.
- Cut in the cold butter using a pastry cutter or fork until the mixture resembles coarse crumbs.
- In a separate bowl, whisk together the heavy cream and vanilla extract.
- Gradually add the cream mixture to the flour mixture, stirring with a fork until a dough forms.

- Turn the dough out onto a lightly floured surface and knead gently until smooth.
- Pat the dough into a 3/4-inch thick circle. Use a round biscuit cutter or cookie cutter to cut out 6-8 biscuits.
- Place the biscuits on the prepared baking sheet and bake for 15-18 minutes, or until golden brown. Remove from the oven and let them cool slightly.

Prepare the Strawberry Filling:
- In a mixing bowl, combine the sliced strawberries, granulated sugar, and lemon juice.
- Toss gently to coat the strawberries in sugar. Let them sit for at least 15-20 minutes to macerate and release their juices.

Make the Whipped Cream:
- In a chilled mixing bowl, whip the chilled heavy cream, powdered sugar, and vanilla extract until stiff peaks form.

Assemble the Strawberry Shortcake:
- Slice the cooled shortcake biscuits in half horizontally.
- Place the bottom halves of the biscuits on serving plates.
- Spoon a generous amount of macerated strawberries over each biscuit bottom.
- Top with a dollop of whipped cream.
- Place the top halves of the biscuits over the whipped cream.
- Garnish with additional strawberries and a dusting of powdered sugar, if desired.

Serve and Enjoy!
- Serve the strawberry shortcake immediately while the biscuits are still slightly warm and the whipped cream is fluffy.
- Enjoy this classic and delightful dessert with fresh strawberries and homemade shortcake biscuits!

Strawberry shortcake is a perfect summer treat that's sure to impress your family and friends. The combination of sweet berries, tender biscuits, and creamy whipped cream creates a heavenly dessert that's irresistible. Enjoy this homemade strawberry shortcake and savor the flavors of summer!